American Genesis

Captain John Smith and the Founding of Virginia

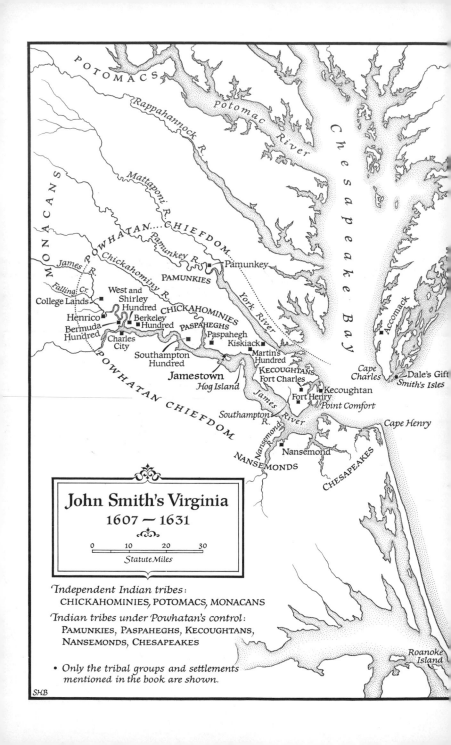

POTOMACS

Rappahannock R.

Potomac River

Chesapeake Bay

Mattaponi R.

POWHATAN CHIEFDOM

MONACANS

James R.

Chickahominy R.

Pamunkey R.

Pamunkey

PAMUNKIES

York River

Accomack

Falling Cr.

College Lands

West and Shirley Hundred

Henrico

Berkeley Hundred

CHICKAHOMINIES

PASPAHEGHS

Bermuda Hundred

Charles City

Paspahegh

Kiskiack

Cape Charles

Dale's Gift

Smith's Isles

Southampton Hundred

Martin's Hundred

KECOUGHTANS

Fort Charles

Jamestown

Hog Island

Fort Henry

Kecoughtan

Point Comfort

POWHATAN CHIEFDOM

James River

Southampton R.

Nansemond R.

Nansemond

Cape Henry

NANSEMONDS

CHESAPEAKES

John Smith's Virginia
1607 — 1631

0   10   20   30

Statute Miles

Independent Indian tribes:
CHICKAHOMINIES, POTOMACS, MONACANS

Indian tribes under Powhatan's control:
PAMUNKIES, PASPAHEGHS, KECOUGHTANS,
NANSEMONDS, CHESAPEAKES

• *Only the tribal groups and settlements
  mentioned in the book are shown.*

Roanoke Island

SHB

Alden T. Vaughan

American Genesis
Captain John Smith and the Founding of Virginia

Edited by Oscar Handlin

Little, Brown and Company · *Boston* · *Toronto*

To Jeff

Credits for illustrations are listed on page 208.

Editor's Preface

To UNDERSTAND AMERICA, it is necessary first to understand Europe. The New World was born in the dreams of the Old.

In the transatlantic relationship, there was always a problem of mistaken identity. What settlers and immigrants expected to find was a product of experience in the places they left. The reality revealed upon arrival was unconnected with that experience and therefore hardly imaginable. For many generations newcomers made the same error John Smith did. They would imagine that the lands beyond the sea existed to remedy the deficiencies of their homelands. Endless surprises awaited them. Much of the early history of America was the product of the divergence between European dream and American actuality.

Elizabethan England had shaped the world of John Smith. He was one of that restless sixteenth-century type who could not stay put. Change, creating heady opportunities for the venturesome, was the rule of his universe. The laggard was quickly out of the race, but lavish prizes rewarded the swift and the daring.

Like many of his contemporaries, Smith early wandered off, first to the east and then to the west. He was a soldier of fortune, literally — living by the use of his sword in the service of whoever would pay. Colonization, for him, was but another employment of the same sort. The chartered companies which launched the overseas ventures of these years needed fighting men to protect their investments. Smith signed on, attracted by the adventurous prospects of a new place, lured by another chance at fortune. He participated in the founding of Virginia as other fighters of his time did in voyages to India, Africa, and Muscovy. His efforts to plant a settlement on the James River were thus the products of English ambition.

Events quickly outran Smith's early dreams. Virginia was no Muscovy or India. Its strange and unexpected environment challenged him to novel reactions. There was no hope of great wealth in the paltry opportunities for trade or booty in that wilderness; men who wished to survive had to work. The indigenous masters of the soil were not such kings and princesses as Smith had met in Hungary or Turkey; he had to learn anew how to deal with the Indians. With these adjustments he took the first steps in transforming a trading post into a permanent, settled society.

After the Captain's departure, Virginia continued upon the course he had set for it. The agricultural system that would develop into the plantation, the black laborers who would become slaves, and the political institutions that would provide a measure of self-government were all in existence by the time he died. His career, therefore, offers a means of surveying some of the dynamic forces at work in early American history.

Alden Vaughan's thoughtful book traces the transformation of the errant dream of a soldier of fortune into an early American social order. By examining the interaction of a vigorous personality and an exciting environment, it throws light both on the man and his time.

OSCAR HANDLIN

Author's Preface

No ENGLISH FLAG waved over an American outpost in 1580, the year of John Smith's birth. Spain controlled thousands of miles of coastline and millions of square miles of the interior. Her armies had already overrun the Aztec civilization in Mexico, the Inca strongholds in Peru, and most of the West Indies. Portugal, enjoying a virtual monopoly on European trade with the Orient, had made little effort to colonize the New World, but she held title to a huge chunk of South America. France possessed no permanent colonies but had explored much of the North American coast and had briefly maintained posts in Florida and Brazil. The Netherlands, engrossed in a struggle for national existence, had not yet entered the American theater, but Dutch holdings in the Far East would soon exceed all but Portugal's. Of Europe's major powers, only England had missed out on the territorial sweepstakes.

By the time of John Smith's death, half a century later, England had footholds around the globe, including several in the New World. With colonies at Virginia, Plymouth, Massachusetts Bay, Bermuda, Barbados, St. Christopher, and other Caribbean islands, and with several more about to be launched, Britain had become a major imperial nation. Henceforth England would dominate the settlement of North America.

This book tells the story of England's belated awakening to the New World's potential and her groping for solutions to the

complex challenge of overseas settlement — problems of organi-
zation, finance, supply, leadership, race relations, and countless
other difficulties. It tells too of the central role played by
Captain John Smith of Lincolnshire and London, who more
than any other man made possible the emergence of British
America. It is not, in the usual sense, a biography of Smith.
His story has already been well told, and as thoroughly as the
limited sources permit. Rather, *American Genesis* treats John
Smith as a symbol of England's early imperial impulse and of
Elizabethan-Jacobean England — a man whose career illus-
trates a formative stage in our national history.

It may be argued that John Smith does not belong in a
Library of American Biography. He was born in England, died
in England, and lived most of his life there. He spent more
years on the European mainland than in America, and he left
no descendants to migrate to the English colonies. But his
credentials as an American are impressive: a member of the
first ruling council in Virginia, and subsequently its president;
the acknowledged savior of the colony during its first two years;
the first and principal historian of Virginia, who also published the earliest and best map of the area; the foremost publicist and cartographer of New England, who gave the area its
name; and a lifelong proponent of English settlement in
America — settlement by sturdy men and women, not get-rich-
quick dandies who would rob the land and head for home.
That he could not end his life in Virginia or New England
was to Smith a matter of profound regret.

I have gleaned the story of Smith and his times from the
scattered sources that have survived the ravages of three and a
half centuries. Unfortunately Smith left only enough information about himself to tantalize us; we have to fill the gaps with
conjecture or remain silent. As historian I dislike weasel words
such as "perhaps," "probably," "maybe," etc., but faithfulness
to the historical record requires occasional caution. I have tried
to let the reader know when I am resorting to educated guesses
and when to demonstrable facts. Although volumes in the

Library of American Biography do not contain footnotes, readers wishing to know the source of any quotation or statement of fact in this book may consult an annotated copy in the library of Columbia University.

To help the reader gain a sense of Smith's era, and to present as accurately as possible the words of the men who founded British America, I have, wherever possible, preserved quotations in their original form, making only a few minor changes (such as interchanging "u" and "v," "i" and "j") to facilitate pronunciation. Sixteenth- and seventeenth-century Englishmen did not care very much how they spelled a word or what punctuation, if any, they used. They cared only for communication, spelling words so they sounded right; an extra letter or variant renditions of the same word did no harm. Neither did random capitalization or erratic use of commas and periods. Smith and his contemporaries cared only that the message got through to the reader. So too, in that sense, do I.

This book has benefitted greatly from critiques by Oscar Handlin, editor of the Library of American Biography, and Philip L. Barbour, the foremost authority on Captain John Smith. I am grateful to both scholars for the generosity with which they shared their time and knowledge.

I am also indebted to several organizations for helping to support my research into early English colonization, of which this book is a preliminary product: the American Council of Learned Societies, the Folger Shakespeare Library, and the Henry E. Huntington Library and Art Gallery. My special thanks to Director James Thorpe and his staff at the Huntington for providing not only an unexcelled collection of manuscript and printed materials but also a rare blend of seclusion and congeniality in which to write.

A. T. V.

Contents

Illustrations

American Genesis

*Captain John Smith
and the Founding of Virginia*

How he slew BONNY·MVLGRO·*Chap·7·*

Capt SMITH *led Captiue to the* BASHAW *of* NALBRITS *in* TARTARIA·*Chap·12·*

Smith   Drub·man   Bashaw

Scenes from John Smith's adventures in Europe and Asia. Top: battling a Turkish soldier; bottom: as a slave in Tartary.

I
Between Two Worlds

SHORTLY BEFORE DAWN on 24 March 1603, the long reign of Elizabeth Tudor ended. Her subjects heard the tolling bells with a mixture of sadness and gratitude, for the Virgin Queen had fashioned a magnificent age. The future looked less promising. James Stuart, her successor, began his regime triumphantly but often failed where she had excelled. Only in the quest for an American empire did he surmount an obstacle that had defied Elizabeth, and even that feat owed less to the new monarch's imagination or skill than to the same dogged persistence that had characterized much of Elizabethan England.

John Smith grew up in Elizabeth's era. Like other schoolboys in the 1580s, he must have listened with youthful awe to tales of the Spanish Armada, wars in Europe, and the exploits — both chivalrous and piratical — of Sir Francis Drake, John Hawkins, and other English seamen. Like many of his contemporaries, too, Smith carried for the rest of his life the era's taste for adventure and achievement.

Elizabethan England knew both. The reigns of Elizabeth's father, her brother Edward, and her sister Mary were profoundly troubled, and the nation again suffered deeply under her distant relatives, the Stuarts of Scotland, who inherited her throne. But for almost half a century England flourished under Elizabeth's benign authority. Some men squabbled over religion, especially the zealous Puritans who resented the Queen's insistence on a Church of England only mildly committed to reformed Protestantism. Other men plotted to swing the Church back to Rome; some even conspired against the Queen's life. For most Englishmen, however, the age of Elizabeth brought unparalleled domestic tranquility. And with peace at home came a fresh opportunity for creativity. William Shakespeare, Christopher Marlowe, and Ben Jonson delighted the public with sophisticated plays; Edmund Spenser, John Donne, and Ben Jonson with superlative poetry; Francis Bacon with brilliant essays; and Sir Walter Ralegh, Raphael Holinshed, and the younger Richard Hakluyt with exciting accounts of history and discovery. Not surprisingly, Elizabethans took abundant — some might call it excessive — pride in their national genius.

What especially endeared the Queen to her subjects was her ability to bring victory when she could not achieve peace. Scotland and France could be mollified; the Puritans and Papists could be outmaneuvered. Spain, however, proved too formidable for any solution but war. Mistrustful of Spanish designs on her throne, Elizabeth sent troops to help the Dutch Republic resist Philip II's attempts to return the Low Countries to subservience and Catholicism. She also let Drake and other "sea dogs" attack Spanish ships and colonies in the West Indies, and she let Ralegh attempt an English outpost on the American coast above the Spanish settlements in Florida. For Spain, the time had come to curb English encroachments. Both nations geared for war. Fortunately for Elizabeth and her people, Philip's "Invincible Armada" faltered before the combined might of the English navy and North Sea tempests. England's decisive victory in 1588 made Elizabeth an untouchable heroine, raised Charles Howard, Francis Drake, and John Hawkins to new heights of popularity, and inspired the entire nation to reassess its role in imperial rivalry.

It was, as Christopher Marlowe observed, "an age of wonder and delight." And not only because of events at home. Throughout the sixteenth century news poured into England from Asia, Africa, and the New World: news of fabulous wealth, of remarkable cures, of extraordinary flora and fauna, of men and women so different from Englishmen as to seem hardly human — strange skin colors, strange customs, strange religions, strange clothing, or none at all. Elizabethans listened incredulously.

Not everything Englishmen heard was true, of course. Some reports were intentionally distorted; others reflected the preconceptions of untrained observers or inaccurate scribes. Almost inevitably, the expectations of their readers led many honest chroniclers — John Smith among them — to exaggerate or to speculate on the basis of meager evidence. But the message was basically true: the world outside England held wonders too vast to comprehend. Most Englishmen remained at home, gradually sifting some truth from the confusing reports. A few men, hardier and more curious than the rest, saw for themselves.

By the time he embarked for America, John Smith had already witnessed more of the world than most of his contemporaries. Too young in the 1580s to participate in England's unsuccessful efforts to plant colonies on the coast of North America, he turned in the next decade toward other lands that captured England's imagination. There he indulged his youthful passion for excitement and bravery; there too he learned some of the lessons and gained some of the perspective that would thrust him into the forefront of England's American venture. Although in 1606 he was the youngest among the leaders of England's first successful colonizing expedition, John Smith was also the most travelled, the most experienced, and the most educated — at least in the practical training more relevant to the conquest of a wilderness than a degree from Oxford or Cambridge. When he joined the expedition to North America, Smith could boast — and probably did — that he had fought more battles, endured more hardships, and seen more strange lands and exotic peoples than any of his companions. Those feats, he discovered later, were an important prologue to the challenges of

America. Toward the end of his life Smith looked back on his adventures in the Old World; "The Warres in *Europe, Asia,* and *Affrica,*" he remembered with characteristic bravado, "taught me how to subdue the wilde Salvages in *Virginia* and *New-England,* in *America.*"

John Smith's beginnings gave little hint of his future. By all the guidelines of his time he should have followed in his father's steps, becoming a yeoman farmer of modest means and limited horizons, and in his early years young Jack complied with that pattern. Born in late 1579 or early 1580 in the small town of Willoughby, Lincolnshire, he attended village schools at nearby Alford and Louth, where he learned the rudiments of English and Latin grammar and a smattering of mathematics. But studies and the prospect of a farmer's life did not appeal to him. Like many a restless lad of his day he dreamed of life at sea. The rolling terrain near Louth, where he lived for some years as a boarding scholar, impressed his expanding mind less than the coastal lowlands of Willoughby with its easy access to the sea. At fifteen John Smith left school to be apprenticed to Thomas Sendall of King's Lynn, a seaport some fifty miles south of Willoughby. Smith later remembered Sendall as "the greatest Merchant of all those parts," and perhaps he was, but by keeping his apprentice landbound the merchant soon lost Smith's services altogether — either by cancellation of the agreement or by Smith's unauthorized departure.

During the next few years, John Smith reshaped his life. He had had enough of formal schooling, enough of sedate vocational training. And with his father's death in 1596 and his mother's remarriage soon after, Smith gained an early independence. Although legally under the control of a guardian, he spent the next five years as independent youths always have: trying one job after another, following his fancies and opportunities in the hope of finding his niche. It was, in short, self-education.

Part of his education came from soldiering. Religious wars kept Europe in turmoil during much of the sixteenth and seventeenth centuries, and every Englishman knew that a major theatre of battle lay just across the channel in the Netherlands. There John Smith, like many of his countrymen, attended "that university of warre, the Lowe Countries," enlisting in 1596 or 1597 with English Protestants fighting the arch-Catholic, Philip II of Spain. Smith served the Dutch cause for two or three years and withdrew only when a lull in the fighting encouraged him to seek adventure elsewhere.

He soon found a new opportunity for education in travel. In the spring of 1599, Peregrine Bertie, lord of Willoughby manor, decided to send his sons Peregrine and Robert on a tour of Europe. By that time Smith had returned to England; an ambitious neighborhood lad with military service to his credit must have impressed Lord Willoughby as a fitting companion. Off Smith went to France to attend the Berties. The position lasted only a short time, for the brothers soon realized that they did not need another servant. But the assignment fed Smith's appetite for seeing the world. Leaving the Berties at Orleans, Smith travelled through Paris to Rouen, and then to Holland where he took ship for Scotland, carrying letters of recommendation to influential Scotsmen who might gain him a post in the court of King James VI. En route Smith experienced his first shipwreck, a portent of his tumultuous future on the sea.

Scotland proved disappointing. Smith failed not only to secure an appointment but also to find any means of support; he returned to Lincolnshire and to soldiering, though now as a student rather than a practitioner. As he recalled in his memoirs (using the fashionable third person), "he retired himselfe into a little wooddie pasture, a good way from any towne. . . . Here by a faire brook he built a Pavillion of boughes, where only in his cloaths he lay. His studie was *Machiavills* Art of warre, and *Marcus Aurelius;* his exercise a good horse, with his lance and Ring. . . ." At the urging of friends he soon acquired a companion, one *"Seignior Thea-dora Polaloga,"* an Italian horseman in the employ of the Earl of Lincoln, who furnished him some of the practical learning not found in books. After mastering a part of the Italian's language, horsemanship, and "good discourse," Smith set off again for the Low Countries. His travels, and his fighting, had barely begun.

European warfare did not satisfy Smith's thirst for glory. Moreover, the fratricidal nature of the battle between Protestant and Catholic bothered him. Largely indifferent to theological issues, Smith preferred the simpler cause of Christ against the infidels. Further east, where Europe and Asia meet, the ancient struggle between Christianity and Islam still raged. In 1600, barely twenty years of age, John Smith decided, as he later recalled, that "he was desirous to see more of the world, and trie his fortune against the *Turkes:* both lamenting and repenting to have seen so many *Christians* slaughter one another." Hungary, he knew, offered that chance.

The long trek to the Hungarian front proved difficult and dangerous. In France Smith fell in with four French "gallants," only to discover that they cared more about fleecing than accompanying him; the rogues soon made off with all his money and baggage. After weeks of frustrating efforts to retrieve his belongings, Smith gained help from the first of a long series of noble ladies who took a liking to the brash young Englishman, and he eventually took ship from Marseilles to Italy. That proved no happy choice either. The passengers were mostly Catholics, "a rabble of Pilgrimes of divers Nations going to *Rome,*" in Smith's opinion; when storms lashed the ship the other voyagers made Smith their scapegoat, cursing him not only as a Protestant but also as an Englishman — "his Nation they swore were all Pyrats" — and threw him overboard. Smith managed to swim to a nearby island where the next day a ship seeking refuge from the storm rescued him. On board a sympathetic Frenchman befriended Smith and supplied him with new clothes and other necessities.

The rescue vessel sailed west across the Mediterranean to the Barbary Coast, then turned eastward. John Smith now caught his first glimpse of Alexandria, Cyprus, Greece, and the Adriatic Coast. And at the entrance to the Adriatic he had his first taste of sea battle. His ship hailed a Venetian vessel which answered with gunfire. He watched the ensuing exchange of broadsides, boardings, fire in the rigging, and at last, surrender of the Italians. Smith probably joined the action; at any rate he shared the spoils of victory for on leaving ship in southern France Smith received about £225 in cash and a little box "worth neere as much more." Comfortably financed now, he moved on through Italy — with a stop in Siena to see the Bertie brothers — to Rome where he watched Pope Clement VIII "creepe up the holy stayres" and say mass at the Church of St. John in Lateran. Smith visited several other Italian cities before crossing into Austria. There he offered his services to Baron Hans Jacob Khissl, Chief of Artillery in the army of Archduke Ferdinand of Austria, who commissioned the Englishman and assigned him to the regiment of "a worthy Collonell, the Earle of Meldritch." At last Smith seemed to have found a role appropriate to his training and his temperament: a soldier of the Lord, locked in mortal combat with the foes of Christendom. Now he could put Machiavelli, Marcus Aurelius, and Seignior Paleologa to the test.

For the next year and a half Smith was all hero. "This *English* Gentleman," as he now styled himself, quickly caught the eyes of his superiors. First he convinced them to try a method of signalling (through a variable arrangement of three torches) between a contingent of the Archduke's army besieged by 20,000 Turks near the Austrian border and the relief army in which Smith served, thus effecting a joint attack by the forces inside and outside the siege lines. Smith also taught General Khissl how to give the Turks a distorted impression of the size of his army by burning thousands of fuses in imitation of lines of musketeers. Both tactics worked to perfection. While the Turks "ranne up and downe as men amazed," the Austrian forces raised the siege in a smashing victory. Smith was promoted to captain and put in command of 250 horsemen.

Not content with these laurels, Smith soon demonstrated that he could capture a city as well as relieve one. For almost sixty years the Turks had held Alba Regalis, "a place so strong by Art and Nature, that it was thought impregnable." If he couldn't go through the defense lines, he could go over them, Smith reasoned. He filled large earthen pots with gunpowder, covered them with pitch mixed with brimstone and turpentine imbedded with quartered musketballs. Over this he put a layer of cloth, then a layer of wick material soaked with linseed oil, camphor, and brimstone. The finished products "he fitly placed in Slings." At midnight Smith ignited "his fiery Dragons" and lofted them into the areas of the town where the Turks were known to gather during attack. Thus distracted, the Turks fell before a well-coordinated assault by several units of the Christian army.

Smith somehow escaped conspicuous heroism in his next battle, an open clash of cavalry forces. He did, however, have a horse killed under him and found himself in the dangerous predicament of combatting on foot against mounted troops. He survived by seizing a riderless horse and so lived to fight another day. And that day, when it came, brought Smith fame and glory. It also brought him a long step toward the armorial insignia (equivalent to an English coat of arms) that would remain a prized possession for the rest of his life. Again a besieged city provided the setting. In the spring of 1602 the Earl of Meldritch slowly began to infiltrate the Turkish defenses at a town Smith called "Regall" (its modern location is uncertain) in southern Transylvania. Bored by the earl's slowness in digging trenches and positioning artillery, the Moslem commander issued a bold if pointless challenge: "That to delight the Ladies, who did long to see some courtlike pastime, the Lord Turbashaw did defie any Captaine, that had the command of a Company, who durst combate with him for his head." Rather than lose face, the earl's officers accepted and drew lots to select their gladiator. Smith won. He won the joust as well, impaling the impetuous Turk with his first thrust. Smith cut off the victim's head as a trophy for his general, left the body to the Turks, and returned unscathed to his cheering army.

Taking Turbashaw's head in no way breached the ethics of battle. It did, however, enrage the Turk's friend, Grualgo, who now "directed a particular challenge to the Conquerour, to regaine his friends head, or lose his owne. . . ." On the next day John Smith returned to the field of honor, armed with lance, pistol, and sword, and again emerged the victor — this time by a well aimed pistol shot that unhorsed his opponent and left him helpless on the ground. Smith took Grualgo's head too.

Then the Englishman became cocky and issued an open challenge to the Turkish army. Bonny Mulgro accepted. But no lances this time; the gladiators fought with pistols, battle axes, and swords. Smith missed with his firearm; by good fortune his combatant missed also. "Their Battle axes was the next," Smith recalled in his memoirs, "whose piercing bils made sometime the one, sometime the other to have scarce sense to keepe their saddles: specially the *Christian* received such a blow that he lost his Battle-axe, and failed not much to have fallen after it; whereat the supposing conquering *Turk,* had a great shout from the Rampiers. The *Turk* prosecuted his advantage to the uttermost of his power; yet the other, what by the readinesse of his horse, and his judgement and dexterity in such a businesse, beyond all mens expectation, by Gods assistance, not onely avoided the *Turkes* violence, but . . . pierced the *Turke* so . . . thorow backe and body, that although he alighted from his horse, he stood not long ere he lost his head, as the rest had done." Captain John Smith, hero of the army of Transylvania and scourge of Islam, received a promotion, a new horse, a sword, a belt worth three hundred ducats, and an embrace from the general. Soon after, the town fell to the Christian forces, which prompted a visit from Prince Zsigmond of Transylvania. Learning of Smith's contributions to this and other victories, and of his feats in single combat, the Prince handsomely rewarded his English soldier: an insignia bearing three Turk's heads, an annual pension of three hundred ducats, and a gilded picture of the Prince.

The siege of Regall marked the high point in Smith's Hungarian career. A few months after the city's fall, the Turks avenged their recent losses. In what John Smith remembered as "this dismall battell," the Transylvanian army at Rottenton suffered, according to Smith's estimate, nearly 30,000 fatalities. They included several English mercenaries who, like Smith, had journeyed far from their homeland "in the defence of *Christ* and his Gospell." Smith too lay among the slaughtered bodies, left for dead. Pillagers found him barely living and, recognizing from his insignia that he must be a man of some prestige, kept him for ransom. Rather than sell their human plunder back to his comrades in the west, however, Smith's captors sent him eastward where laborers commanded a good price.

Thus began the brief but painful career of John Smith, slave. With other captives he was displayed, he recalled, "like beasts in a market-place," where prospective buyers "viewing their limbs and wounds, caused slaves to struggle with them, to trie their strength." Smith soon became the property of one Bashaw Bogall who sent him along with other bondsmen to Constantinople; "by twentie and twentie chained by the neckes" they marched the five hundred miles to the great Moslem city. There Smith's luck improved briefly; he became a household slave to Charatza Tragabigzanda (Smith's spelling; we have nothing else to go on), a mistress of his new owner. This lady took a liking to the Englishman and through a common knowledge of Italian she learned of his origin and adventures. His story aroused her sympathy and her ire, for the Bashaw had falsely described Smith as a Bohemian lord whom he had captured in battle. In a futile attempt to be kind, Lady Tragabigzanda sent Smith to her brother in Tartary, accompanied by an appeal for good treatment. She hoped Smith would fare well until she could find a way to protect him or to free him outright.

Her brother had other ideas. No sooner did Smith arrive in Tartary than he was stripped naked, his head and beard shaved, and an iron ring rivetted around his neck. No special treatment for the Englishman; he shared the hard labor, meager diet, and comfortless circumstances of his fellow-slaves — Christians, Turks, and Moors — "and he being the last, was slave of slaves to them all."

There seemed little hope of relief. Lady Tragabigzanda would not know of his plight; the other slaves insisted that escape was impossible; and the odds of his being ransomed by a Christian agent — rare but not unknown — appeared slim. Then came an unexpected chance. Assigned to thresh grain on a distant field, Smith one day found himself alone with his master who used the occasion to "beat, spurne, and revile" the Englishman. Instinctively Smith struck back, using his thresher as a club. The first blow was fatal. Smith hid the body under some straw, donned his oppressor's clothes, and galloped off on the Tartar's horse "he knew not whither." A few days of wandering brought him to a main thoroughfare where he could tell the way to Muscovy, for at each intersection the arms of the signposts carried symbols of the destinations: "if towards the *Georgians* and *Persia,* a blacke man, full of white spots; if toward China, the picture of a Sunne; if towards Muscovia, the sign of a Crosse. . . ."

For sixteen days, according to his later recollection, Smith followed the signposts, ever fearful of being identified as a runaway by the iron around his neck, by his shaved head, or by his obvious unfamiliarity with the land and language. Somehow the resourceful Englishman played his role convincingly enough to reach a Russian garrison on the River Don, where the Christian governor took off his irons. There too, as Smith reported cryptically, "the good *Lady Callamata,*" latest in his string of women saviours, "largely supplied all his wants."

That was in 1603. Smith had seen more of the world than any Lincolnshire farmboy could plausibly dream about. His thirst for excitement had been sated for the moment; it was time to go home. Armed with a certificate of safe passage from the Russian governor, Smith joined a caravan heading west.

A direct journey home would have been out of character. Smith's path led through Muscovy, Lithuania, and Poland, then into Transylvania where he found many of his old friends and comrades-in-arms. "In all his life," Smith wrote of the return trip, "he seldome met with more respect, mirth, content, and entertainment. . . ." He lingered only briefly in Transylvania, for Prince Zsigmond and the Earl of Meldritch were not there, and Smith could not quit their service without permission. "Being thus glutted with content, and neere drowned with joy," he pushed on through Hungary to Prague and then to Leipzig where he at last found his commanders. From the Prince he received a written version of his insignia, a release from further military service, and 1500 gold ducats (worth more than £500) in lieu of his annual pension and in consideration of his recent hardships. Reluctant to leave Europe without seeing some of its fabled cities, Smith travelled through Germany, with stops at Dresden, Wittenberg, and Munich; on through France where he visited Paris, Orleans, and Nantes; then by ship to Spain to see Valladolid, Toledo, Cordova, and Seville. Close to Africa, and "satisfied with *Europe* and *Asia*," Smith could not resist the temptation to see more of the continent he had glimpsed from shipboard three years before. From Gibraltar he sailed to North Africa.

There too Smith found excitement. He had barely reached the Moroccan Coast when he took passage on a French man-of-war. Forced by storms into the Atlantic, the Frenchmen seized an opportunity to prey on Spanish shipping near the Canary Islands before heading back to the coast of Africa. In a battle with two Spanish men-of-war, graphically described in later years by Captain Smith, the three vessels exchanged broadsides and small shot for two days. Eventually the Spaniards boarded the French ship and set it on fire, but after a fierce struggle the Frenchmen repelled their boarders, doused the fires, and slipped away. Smith did not say whether he took part in the hand-to-hand combat, but it is hard to picture him a mere spectator. More likely he played the role of privateer, wielding a sword with vigor and skill despite his lack of official ties to the French navy. In either case, the battle fittingly climaxed four years of adventure. As soon as the warship reached port, Smith found passage to England.

During Smith's absence, England had changed in ways that would influence his life profoundly. More important even than the passing of the Queen and the accession of James Stuart was the revived interest in America, an interest that had long lain dormant and that had thus far escaped John Smith's attention.

Since the days of Marco Polo, and later of Christopher Columbus, Vasco da Gama, and Ferdinand Magellan, nations of western Europe had gained a sense of opportunity and optimism in distant lands. They had earlier suffered chagrin and despair, even self-doubt, at the failure of their crusades against Islam. The discoveries of the late fifteenth and early sixteenth centuries dispelled that mood as sudden access to new lands and new peoples revived Europe's craving for material and spiritual gain. Like crusaders of old, Christian men set forth to find gold and spices and precious cloth and to reap harvests of new converts.

Until the age of Elizabeth, few Englishmen shared Europe's discoveries. England's troubles kept her people at home. The Hundred Years' War against France dragged on until 1453; it was soon followed by a devastating struggle between the houses of York and Lancaster that did not end until 1485 when Henry Tudor prevailed over Richard III at Bosworth Field. Intermittent warfare against Scotland and later against

France lasted well into the sixteenth century. Then came religious turmoil under Henry VIII and his heirs that halted only in 1558 with the accession of Elizabeth. Within three years the new Queen achieved peace with France and Scotland and eased England's theological discord by a skillful compromise of traditional and reformist elements.

Until then, England had made only one significant probe to the west. In 1497 Henry VII commissioned John and Sebastian Cabot to seek a northern passage to the Orient. When that goal eluded them, and when the land they touched revealed no immediate wealth, the House of Tudor lost interest. (The "right" of first discovery, however, remained a future basis for English exploration and settlement because the Cabots had reached the North American mainland a year before Columbus's third voyage entered the Gulf of Mexico.) For the next eighty years English vessels and English seamen appeared only occasionally along the American coast. Henry VIII knighted Sebastian Cabot, and Edward VI conferred a pension on the aging explorer; neither monarch sent expeditions to America.

What the Tudor kings had failed to exploit, Queen Elizabeth attempted. Partly to pull the Spanish tail, partly to find new revenue for her royal coffers, in 1576 she sent Martin Frobisher in search of a northwest passage. He, of course, failed too, but his optimistic reports of a northern route to China and a widespread belief that he had found gold stimulated enough enthusiasm to finance two more trips. (The wish for gold proved father to the thought; the 200 tons of yellow ore that Frobisher placed for safekeeping in the Tower of London turned out to be nothing but American dirt.) But gold or not, English interest in discovery mounted rapidly.

Two men now entered the scene who between them reshaped England's imperial role. One, the dashing nobleman Sir Walter Ralegh, put in motion the first English efforts at colonization. The other, the studious clergyman-anthologist Richard Hakluyt, made England understand their importance. Neither man took part in the actual settlement of America, though Ralegh once tried to plant a colony in South America. But they, and others like them — including Hakluyt's older cousin of the same name, an attorney and geographer who introduced the younger Richard to the wonders of the expanding world — aroused Englishmen from "their sluggish security." Ralegh's contribution lay in organization, in gathering the necessary authority, funds, and supplies for expeditions of discovery and settlement. Meanwhile Hakluyt's essays and his voluminous compilations of exploration narratives convinced the Crown and the public that England must take her rightful place among the empires that bridged the Old World to the New.

Hakluyt saw what had escaped most of his countrymen: England had much to gain in America even if there should be no northwest passage to navigate and no golden cities to plunder. In 1582 — John Smith was only two years old — Hakluyt published his first collection of exploration narratives, prefaced with an appeal for a vigorous English colonizing effort. Some years before, Elizabeth had been interested enough in expansion to grant Ralegh's half-brother, Sir Humphrey Gilbert, a six-year monopoly on New World settlement. Gilbert squandered his fortune, and his wife's, on an outpost in frigid Newfoundland, assuming, as many others did, that the climate of North America paralleled that of Europe. Trouble beset his efforts from the outset, and in the end destroyed him when his flagship foundered in an Atlantic storm. The Queen agreed to let her subjects try again, but not with her money.

In 1584, Hakluyt's "Discourse Concerning Western Planting" urged Elizabeth to support Ralegh's imperialistic schemes. He argued that North America was there for the taking, easily reached by routes that did not directly threaten the occupied territory of any other Christian monarch. (The rights of heathens, Hakluyt assumed, did not matter.) Spain might object, but never mind. One of the principal aims of English colonization would be to thwart King Philip, both in his American possessions and in his Pacific empire. English America, Hakluyt predicted, would be a base of operations against England's most formidable rival. It would also be a base for the advancement of "sincere religion" against the "scarlet whore," as Protestants irreverently dubbed the Church of Rome. And when settled with sturdy Englishmen, an empire in America would offer much: a market for English goods; a source of masts, pitch, and other naval supplies; and a new home for England's poor and unemployed.

The removal of England's poor had great appeal to her gentry. During the last years of Elizabeth's reign, economic depression and burgeoning population combined with a decline of small farms to create two alarmingly large and often disorderly classes. First, the honest poor who could not find work or suffered from disabling afflictions, and second, the willful poor — "the theefe, the Rogue, the Strumpet, the sturdy Beggar, the Filcher, the Couzener, Cut-purse, and such like." Or so a great many preachers and pamphleteers believed in the late sixteenth and early seventeenth centuries. They watched with dismay as swelling masses of humanity threatened the purity and orderliness of English society. With no jobs to occupy their time and thoughts, the idle poor became a devil's playground: they "seeke out disordered Alehouses, where they sweare and forsweare, Banne, Curse, Blaspheme God, disdaine good things, slander and backbite their Neighbors, use all unlawfull Exercises. . . . [L]ike Catepillars, Waspes, and Droanes, they eate and devoure uppe the Fruites and sweet Commodities of the Commonwealth." London, especially, attracted the dispossessed. That great city of more than a quarter-million inhabitants, the center of England's government, commerce, and art, had become in the eyes of many spokesmen a refuge for all of society's outcasts and criminals — "abounding in all kinds of filthinesse and prophanenesse."

America offered the perfect solution. God had ordered man to multiply and fill the earth, and the New World appeared to

Englishmen a vast, empty continent. A few natives lived there, to be sure, but they posed no problem. As heathens they *needed* Christian neighbors (Anglican of course) from whom they might learn the glories of the true faith. The Indians simply would not, and could not, offer much resistance to well-intentioned Englishmen. Were not the colonists coming with an olive branch in one hand and the Gospel in the other? Clergyman William Symonds summed up the situation as his generation saw it. There's "a difference" he insisted, "between a bloody invasion and the planting of a peaceable Colony in a waste country, where the people doe live but like Deere in heards, and . . . have not as yet attained unto the first modestie that was in *Adam*. . . ."

The promoters of colonization appealed not only to the Englishman's patriotism and moral obligations to heathens and his own unfortunate compatriots, but also to his avarice. The prospects of gold and silver could not be entirely dismissed, and even if none were found in the English sphere, the promise remained of high returns on less dramatic resources: on crops, skins, silk, wool, or iron ore; on the more obvious naval stores; and on salted fish. Reverend Daniel Price predicted that it would become "the *Barne of Britaine* . . . the *Garden* of the World." America, in short, offered something for everyone, whether settlers, investors, or merely Englishmen whose sole interest lay in a less crowded and more orderly mother country.

It was one thing to convince Englishmen that America was worth the effort, quite another to marshall that effort effectively. With little experience in colonization and only the model of arch-enemy Spain to emulate or reject, England for a time floundered badly in the practical pursuit of an American empire. Then Sir Walter Ralegh took hold. Despite the Queen's reluctance to invest in his expeditions (he named England's sector of the American mainland for the Virgin Queen anyway), Ralegh in 1584 sent a scouting expedition to find a suitable location for a colony; it returned with valuable information and two American natives. The next year Ralegh sent his cousin, Sir Richard Grenville, with three ships to Roanoke Island off the coast of North Carolina. While Grenville sailed back to England, one hundred men under Ralph Lane began to build England's first outpost in America; when their supplies ran low and Grenville failed to reappear, however, they accepted Sir Francis Drake's offer of passage home. Ralegh's first attempt had lasted less than a year.

His subsequent efforts had even less success. Grenville left fifteen men at Roanoke in 1586. By the time the next expedition arrived a year later, all fifteen had disappeared, presumably slaughtered by the Indians. This third contingent, including several women and the infant Virginia Dare, born on the island, also vanished by the time Ralegh sent a relief ship in 1590. America, it seemed, had as much potential for disaster as for profits and national glory. The Roanoke failures dampened the spirits and closed the pocketbooks of the few in England who could finance New World colonization. Neither the Crown nor wealthy nobles would take such a risk again. Some other solution must be found.

That solution had, in fact, been maturing slowly in Elizabethan England and merely awaited application to the matter in hand. Since the mid-sixteenth century Englishmen had invested extensively in overseas ventures through regulated commercial companies to which the Crown granted trade monopolies in return for a percentage of the profits. In this manner England expanded her commerce into Russia, Turkey, the Mediterranean, and along the African Coast. But such companies functioned almost as guilds, with membership strictly limited and profits narrowly apportioned; their objective lay more in orderly trade than in expanding opportunities for England's swelling middle class. By the dawn of the seventeenth century an important new type of corporation had evolved. Also chartered by the Crown, but free of the stifling regulations of the earlier organizations, joint-stock companies opened membership to anyone who could afford a relatively inexpensive share; in return the investors helped to shape company policy and reaped rewards in proportion to the money "adventured." Subscriptions could be for single voyages or for longer-term projects.

The same techniques could apply equally well to colonization. Investors would risk little for a chance at great profits; the Crown would contribute a charter of monopoly to explore and settle a specified area in return for the satisfaction of enriching the empire; officers of the companies would contribute their energy and talent in order to wield power and influence. The expenses of settlement — for ships, crews, salaries, trading goods, tools, weapons — would be widely shared. So long as public confidence, and therefore the amounts invested, remained high, and so long as the urge to make money did not overshadow the needs of the settlers themselves, the joint-stock company promised England a way to plant colonies at minimal risk to both the government and the people. In 1606 the theory awaited a practical test.

John Smith came home just as the new wave of interest in America broke upon the English people. His timing could not have been better, for the first years of the seventeenth century saw the formation of new companies and the emergence of new leaders, among whom Smith soon took his place.

England's New World ventures had made little progress from 1590, when Sir Walter Ralegh ceased to be active in colonization, until 1602. That year, only two years before Smith's return, three English explorers sailed for North America: Samuel Mace to the southern coast, Bartholomew Gosnold to the northern part, and George Waymouth in search of a northwest passage. Other voyages followed in 1603 and 1605. In the latter year Waymouth returned from his second voyage to America with five Indians; the curiosity they aroused and the favorable reports of his sailors kindled fresh enthusiasm for a colonizing effort. Within a year two groups of knights and merchants — one centered in London, the other in the West Country ports of Plymouth, Bristol, and Exeter — petitioned the Crown for authority to establish outposts in America. "Mostly at the urging of Richard Hakluyt, who has industriously described all the remote voyages of the English," King James in April, 1606 chartered two corporations, a northern (generally referred to as the Plymouth Company) and a southern (known as the London Company) with exclusive rights to part of the American mainland. A royal council of thirteen would watch over the activities of both companies while day-to-day management would rest in the corporations themselves. The charter left on-site government of the colonies to resident councils selected by the parent organizations. John Smith had no hand in the petitions nor did his name appear in the King's grant. He undoubtedly heard rumors, though, of the charter's progress through the royal bureaucracy and watched for a chance to join the enterprise. Since his return in 1604 he had become curious to see "the unknown parts of uncivilized *America*."

During the next year or two, observant Londoners may have noticed a short, muscular man with bristling moustache and a full, round beard (not the aristocratic pointed style) pushing through the city's crowded docks or probing its boisterous taverns in search of an expedition to America. In 1605 he signed with a group preparing to explore the Oyapock River in South America; when its leader died the voyage was cancelled, leaving Smith to cast about for other employment. Again his timing was propitious. Bartholomew Gosnold, a principal organizer of the London Company and a relative of the Berties, needed leaders for an expedition to Chesapeake Bay. Gosnold must have heard of Smith's exploits, and recruited him — without too much difficulty. Smith may also have been encouraged by Richard Hakluyt, a charter member of the company, whose works had a lifelong influence on the captain. Or perhaps he attended a performance of *Eastward Hoe* at Blackfriars theatre where he would have heard "Seagull" boast that "golde is more plentifull [in Virginia] then copper is with us; . . . Why, man, all their dripping-pans and their chamber-potts are pure gould; and all the chaines with which they chaine up their streets are massie gold; all the prisoners they take are fetered in gold; and for rubies and diamonds they goe forth on holydayes and gather 'hem by the sea-shore to hang on their childrens coates, and sticke in their children's caps. . . . You shall live freely there, without sargeants, or courtiers, or lawyers, or intelligencers. . . ."

That must have whetted Smith's appetite. And what better choice for a robust, restless knight errant than an expedition, in the words of poet Michael Drayton,

> To get the Pearle and Gold,
> And ours to hold,
> VIRGINIA
> Earth's onely Paradise. . . .

*The European expected America's wealth
to fall into his hands.*

I I

Outpost

On Friday, 19 December 1606, John Smith boarded ship at Blackwall, London. By nightfall most of the other passengers and crewmen had crowded into the hundred-ton flagship *Susan Constant* and her smaller escorts, the forty-ton *Godspeed* and twenty-ton *Discovery;* early next morning they slipped down the Thames and made their way to the east coast of England. There contrary winds, the frequent bane of expeditions to America, held them in sight of land for six weeks. Before the small squadron finally sailed into blue water its provisions had been partly exhausted, its preacher lay perilously ill, and bitter quarreling had broken out among the passengers — an inauspicious start for England's new effort to colonize America.

Once at sea, Smith and his companions faced an arduous and circuitous trip to Virginia. The preferred trans-Atlantic route of the early seventeenth century led southward to the Canary Islands, then southwest to a point off the African coast where the north equatorial current flowed to the West Indies; from there ships could ride the Gulf Stream up the coast of North America. That route had the advantage of generally fair winds, relatively short hauls between ports, and confidence engendered by a familiar path. The disadvantage was duration: a journey of more than five thousand miles took from twelve to twenty weeks. At best colonists reached their destinations low on energy and ill-prepared to resist unfamiliar diseases; at worst the ships ran out of food and water, or epidemics struck on the high seas. Smith's shipmates knew many tales of disaster. They realized too that on arrival in America they faced the likelihood of illness or violent death. Yet they pushed on, encouraged by the hope that this expedition, unlike others, would survive and prosper.

It did survive, but not without a heavy share of the hardships that accompanied most seventeenth-century ocean crossings. The voyagers endured abysmally cramped quarters in low-ceilinged cabins with foul air and no privacy. They subsisted on barely edible rations: scant portions of salted meat and fish, stale biscuits, rancid cheese and butter, and beer of dubious quality — while it lasted. Long voyages never had enough fresh water for drinking and cooking. (One of the travellers later recalled that on his trip back to England the water "was so stencheous thatt . . . I cold nott endure the sentt thereof.") Seasickness racked many of the passengers. Others suffered more serious illnesses, while nutritional deficiencies drained human energy and spirit. So did the monotony of week after endless week of inaction, eased only by petty chores and an occasional exchange of rumors or tall tales. For more than four months the Virginia expedition pitched and rolled across the Atlantic; brief stops at the Canaries and at some of the Caribbean Islands offered temporary relief and fresh food. Almost everyone survived — only one man is known to have died among the more than one hundred fifty prospective colonists and crewmen — but the frightful mortality of the first years at Jamestown bore poignant testimony to the human cost of colonization.

Command of the expedition rested in Captain Christopher Newport of *Susan Constant,* a veteran of sea dog raids on the Spanish West Indies, whose missing arm evoked bitter reminders of the New World's perils. Commanding the other ships were Bartholomew Gosnold, equally experienced in American waters, in *Godspeed;* and John Ratcliffe, about whom little is known except that he had a penchant for trouble, in *Discovery*. In Virginia the three captains would share leadership of the colony with Edward Maria Wingfield, a veteran soldier and the only settler named in the royal charter; Captain John Martin, a soldier and lawyer; Captain George Kendall, another troublemaker; George Percy, a veteran of the Low Countries and youngest brother of the Earl of Northumberland; and John Smith. Newport would stay only briefly. The company expected him to load a saleable cargo and return to England.

There is no complete roster of the men who composed the expedition of 1606–1607, but partial lists published later by John Smith reveal that it included more than fifty gentlemen, among them Reverend Robert Hunt, the only clergyman; also four carpenters, twelve laborers, two bricklayers, a blacksmith, a mason, a tailor, a surgeon, a sailmaker, a drummer, and four boys, with, one account concludes, "diverse others, to the number of 105." These were "the first planters"; not included in that category were the ships' crews and perhaps some disgruntled passengers who went back to England with the return voyage. The list throws little light, however, on the character of the first settlers. The enterprise called for men of skill, energy, and self sacrifice; from what is known of the events of the first few years, both the leaders and the followers fell far short of that mark. Virginia survived not because of its first settlers but in spite of them.

A case in point is the attempt in mid-voyage to discredit John Smith and — if we can believe his account — to execute him before he even set foot in America. Details of the episode are shrouded by sparse and conflicting evidence, but the outline is clear. By the time the expedition reached the Canaries, Smith was under arrest; when it stopped at Nevis in the West Indies for food and recreation, Smith's enemies were ready to hang him from a hastily constructed gallows, "but Captaine *Smith,* for whom they were intended, could not be perswaded to use them." What caused such fear and hatred of Smith is hard to detect. Seventeenth-century Englishmen thought they saw plots everywhere, not always unreasonably, and it would have taken little to convince the sea-weary voyagers that Captain Smith had dangerous intentions. He may have tried to shorten the months at sea by spinning tales of his own adventures, which, however true, could only have struck some of his hearers as incredible and must have aroused deep resentment among the gentlemen on board. They knew, as did the lesser folk, that the gentry would rule the colony. But how could gentlemen command respect when a yeoman's son bragged of credentials far more valid in a land of hostile natives and unknown perils than proper breeding or connections at Court? Perhaps some of Smith's new acquaintances began to whisper too loudly that they would cleave to him if the going got rough. According to an account later published in Smith's *Map of Virginia,* fault lay with "some of the chiefe (envying his repute) ; who fained he intended to usurpe the governement, murder the Councell, and make himselfe king." In any event, Smith escaped the gallows because Captain Newport refused to hang a man without more evidence. Newport kept him under arrest, his case to be determined in Virginia.

By late April the three small ships had reached the latitude of Chesapeake Bay, almost in sight of land, when "God, the guider of all good actions, forc[ed] them by an exteam storme . . . to their desired port. . . ." They arrived none too soon. Captain Ratcliffe of *Discovery* already counselled return to England. Now, with the ocean crossing behind them, this latest contingent of Englishmen could begin the job they had been sent to do: to create in the American wilderness an outpost of British power and Christian civilization. That, at least, was their reputed mission. Most of the passengers had more mundane objectives: to get a fat share of Virginia's reputed riches and to enjoy for a while the American Garden of Eden.

The more realistic passengers, including John Smith, had doubts about easy wealth and easy living. Almost matching reports of the New World's grandeur were tales of its pitfalls: horrendous storms, deadly plants, ferocious animals, and man-eating natives. The Indians painted by artist-governor John White at Roanoke appeared peaceful, but they lived farther south and did not belong to the tribes of the Chesapeake region. Similarly, the Roanoke settlers had found fertile soil, but they had been in a different locality. No European had explored extensively the area Newport's men were about to settle; its benign reputation rested on sparse reports. Closer examination might reveal unexpected terrors. The Virginia colonists therefore felt anxiety as well as hope; some perhaps harbored silent fears, especially when pondering the mysterious fate of the Roanoke colony.

Belief that the Virginia venture would succeed where others had failed hinged partly on geography — Chesapeake Bay was expected to be a far better location; and partly on diplomacy — this colony would treat the Indians kindly, Captain Newport resolved. His intention received an early jolt: when he took a party ashore at Cape Henry (which he tactfully named for the Prince of Wales), a band of Indians assaulted the English, wounding two of them "very dangerously." Confident that other Indians would be friendlier and that the interior would fulfill earlier predictions, Newport led his squadron across the bay and up the nearest large river. After some preliminary exploration the leaders found an acceptable spot to unload and begin settlement. There, on 13 May 1607, the resident councillors, whose names had been brought in a sealed box to prevent jealousies en route and to avoid undercutting Captain Newport's authority at sea, took their oaths of office. The London Company had named seven men: Newport, Gosnold, Ratcliffe, Wingfield, Martin, Kendall, and Smith. In its first official act the resident council voted to have Wingfield its president and to exclude Smith, still under suspicion.

The council's assignment was formidable. It had, first of all, to force a disparate collection of Englishmen to work in harmony lest they perish — no small task in light of the settlers' obstinate individualism and the forest's abundant perils. Moreover, the council had to meet the company's demand for profits. The London Company had hired men to build an outpost where the discovery of gold, trade with the Indians, or the raising of crops would bring a fair return on the stockholders' investment. After seven years the settlers would be given land, plus other benefits, and could do more or less as they pleased. In the meantime they worked for the company; in return they received passage, food, shelter (which they, of course, must build), and protection (which they must provide). They would labor as the company directed, be fed from its storehouse, live in its communal lodgings, and worship in accordance with its ecclesiastical preferences. Such conditions did not have wide appeal, and some of the men who accepted them in England changed their minds after a few weeks in Virginia. But they had made a bargain and must live up to it — if the council could make them.

Despite the wrangling over Smith's place on the council and the discouraging first encounter with American Indians, prospects for success were bright in the early months. The country appeared bountiful, the climate salubrious. Observers compared the weather in Virginia to that of balmy Spain. Chesapeake Bay itself offered shelter from ocean tempests, yet with an entrance nearly twenty miles wide it promised ready access to the interior. Into the bay flowed "5. faire and delightful navigable rivers" of which they named the southernmost after the King. And no doubt the James River seemed majestic to Englishmen who were familiar only with smaller streams. It could be followed by a ship of three hundred tons for one hundred and fifty miles inland; its breadth of one half to two miles allowed easy navigation. Everywhere seafood flourished in startling size and abundance: sturgeon up to seven feet in length, great crabs that four men could feed on, as well as oysters, mussels, and an almost endless variety of saltwater fish, including one "like the picture of St. *George* his Dragon."

The land was equally generous. Near the mouth of the river "fayre pyne trees" promised pitch and tar; further inland the larger trees could be cut into clapboard, timber, and masts, or when cleared would give way to fertile gardens. And throughout the dense forests roamed an amazing array of fowl and fur-bearing animals, some of which the Englishmen had never seen: raccoons "almost as big as a *Fox*, as good meat as a lamb," and opossums "of the bignesse and likenesse of a Pigge, of a moneth ould, a beast of as strange as incredible nature. . . ." "Suche a Baye, a Ryvar and a land," wrote William Brewster, one of the gentlemen settlers, "did nevar the eye of mane behould."

What the settlers beheld, however, did not quite satisfy them. The hated Spaniards had found gold and silver; Englishmen would settle for no less. And at first Virgnia appeared to hold riches of infinite value. "If we maye beleve ether in wordes or Letters," Sir Walter Cope reported to Secretary of State Salisbury shortly after Captain Newport's return to England, "we are falne upon a lande, that promises more then the Lande of promisse: In steed of mylke we finde pearle. / & golde Inn steede of honye. Thus they saye, thus they wryte." Cope, in England, had doubts about the mineral riches, as did Smith in Virginia. But they were exceptions. Englishmen on both sides of the Atlantic clung tenaciously to their greedy hopes, swallowing every Indian tale of precious metals. The mountains above the falls, most of the settlers and the adventurers back home believed, "prommyseth Infynyt treasuer." Newport himself lent credence to the rumors by insisting to Lord Salisbury that Virginia was "verie Riche in gold and Copper."

Had the chimera of gold been merely an idle hope, no harm would have been done except to individual expectations. But the search for gold involved time and energy that other projects sorely needed. "There was no talke, no hope, no worke," Smith complained, "but dig gold, wash gold, refine gold, loade gold. . . ." Smith recognized the "guilded durt" for what it was. He realized too that the men could not live indefinitely in tents, nor could they exist for long on the scanty supplies they had brought along. And however plentiful the rivers and forests seemed at first view, the settlers had neither the tools nor the skill to feed themselves exclusively on fish and game. Worse still, the lust for valuable metals so dazzled the London Company that it included in the first supply expedition several appallingly irrelevant artisans: two goldsmiths, two refiners, a jeweler, and a perfumer. Virginia needed builders and tillers of the soil; it got gentlemen and practitioners of aristocratic crafts.

The quest for quick riches unfortunately coincided with another fundamental error: the selection of Jamestown as the principal seat of the new colony. At first glance the choice seemed sound enough. Situated fifty-seven miles up river from the ocean, the narrow-necked peninsula, virtually an island, offered relative safety from incursions by Spanish or French warships. At the very least an enemy fleet would be spotted long before it could reach the settlement. Jamestown's peninsular location also protected the settlers against Indian attacks from the mainland, though at first the fifteen-hundred-acre tract was too large to defend; for many years English settlement covered only a small corner of the island. Defense, then, was a major consideration but not the only one. More important, tall pines close to the shore and the deep channel of the river at that point permitted ships to be tied up to the banks, thus dispensing with the laborious task of loading and unloading by small boats. And situated more than a third of the way to the fall line, the island would become a convenient point from which to send search parties for gold.

More than offsetting Jamestown's advantages was its threat to health. The colonists had fortunately arrived in mid-May, probably the most comfortable season in the area, and thus had not noticed the potential dangers of their location. Besides, an almost endless list of tasks needed immediate attention. As one settler reported, the colonists "falleth every man to worke, the Councell contrive the Fort, the rest cut downe trees to make place to pitch their Tents; some provide clap-

board to relade the ships; some make gardens, some nets, etc."
Within a few weeks the settlers had sown fields of wheat,
constructed a few crude buildings and loaded *Susan Constant*
and *Godspeed* with clapboard, sassafras roots ("our easiest
and richest comodity" because of its reputation as a cure for
syphilis and other maladies), and samples of ore. Intent on
their labors and lulled by congenial weather, the colonists
failed to notice that they inhabited an unhealthy swamp and
that the brackish water they drank would eventually undermine their stamina. For the moment, however, they had energy
enough. On 22 June 1607 the two ships, Captain Newport
again in command, set sail for England. He left behind
approximately one hundred men and several boys, and the
pinnace *Discovery*. The colonists appeared in good health and
spirits and eager to continue exploring the mainland.

Ten days later only a handful were well. Disease hit with
frightening suddenness, brought on by a crippling combination of hot weather, hard work, foul water, and skimpy diet.
Gone were the meat and ale to which husky Elizabethan
appetites were accustomed; daily rations now consisted of half
a pint of wheat and as little of barley, both wormy from
months at sea. Even the kegs of hard tack were empty; sailors
before their departure had pilfered them from the ships'
storage and sold the precious biscuits to unwary settlers who
had too little foresight to save for the lean months ahead. In
August the death rate climbed alarmingly. Captain Smith
later recalled that "God (being angrie with us) plagued us
with such famin and sicknes that the living were scarce able to
bury the dead. . . ."

By September half the company had died, including
Bartholomew Gosnold. A few had fallen victim to Indian
arrows, a few had succumbed to the immediate effects of
inadequate diet, and one had been executed for treason. Most
died from infections to which English bodies had little im-
munity, especially after a rugged year of travel, work, and
malnutrition. John Smith took ill but recovered, probably

because his earlier life had exposed him to a wide range of diseases.

Then came winter. In both Europe and America an unusually heavy frost lasted from late 1607 to early 1608. Frozen feet and chilblains joined the growing list of ailments. On the second day of the new year Captain Newport arrived with 120 new, but equally unacclimated, settlers and badly needed supplies. Still misfortune plagued the colony. On January 7 fire raced through its huddled cottages, burning the storehouse and all but three of the dwellings, and indirectly causing further mortality among the ill and the newly arrived. When spring brought respite from the cold and the end of the first year at Jamestown, only 38 of the original 105 colonists still lived.

Spring also brought another load of settlers. In April Captain Nelson, who had left England the previous fall with Newport, but separated from him by foul weather had wintered in the West Indies, brought *Phoenix* into port with more mouths to feed. Better preparations and a less wearing voyage helped to reduce the mortality among the newest colonists, yet between the spring and fall of 1608 death claimed another thirty victims, most of them from Nelson's ship. In the first eighteen months Jamestown had lost almost half its inhabitants.

The danger of Indian attack vied with malnutrition and disease as the greatest threat to the survival of the English colony. The Indians, in all probability, had exterminated the brief footholds on Roanoke Island; now they seemed likely to doom the Virginia experiment as well, unless they could be persuaded to help rather than hinder the effort.

Early contacts proved inconclusive. Despite some scattered clashes many peaceful meetings had taken place. After the initial skirmish on Cape Henry, the Indians greeted the Englishmen cordially, feasting the newcomers and giving them tobacco and other symbols of friendship. Even the few who seemed unhappy at the foreigners' intrusion succumbed to kindness. While scouting for a place to settle in early May the expedition encountered "many stout and able Savages . . . in a most warlike manner, with the swords at their backes beset with sharpe stones, and pieces of yron able to cleave a man in sunder." Yet when the Indians "demanded of us our being there, willing us to bee gone," the English gave signs of amity, and in the end the natives "let us land in quietnesse."

During the next few weeks relations vacillated. Part of the problem lay in the rivalries and conflicting interests of the various tribes. The hostility of some encouraged others to make peace with the white men; conversely, the friendship of some Indians assured the enmity of others. There were problems of communication too, stemming in many cases from the language barrier that throughout the seventeenth century proved insurmountable to all but a few of either race. And the cultural gap was even more formidable. There were striking contrasts in religion, in political structure, in economic systems, as well as lesser matters of clothing, hair styles, and eating habits. The significance of these and other differences would grow, rather than diminish, with time. For now, each race merely viewed with suspicion the other's customs. The English, for example, expressed astonishment and dismay at what they considered the indolence of Indian men and the drudgery of Indian women; the natives thought Englishmen performed "effemynate labour."

In spite of cultural and linguistic impediments, Newport persisted in allaying Indian distrust of the English, for a while even limiting fortification at Jamestown to a half moon of branches. The folly of that tactic became apparent in early June when two hundred warriors attacked the outpost, killing an English boy and wounding perhaps a score of the men. At the time, Newport, Smith, and twenty-two others were exploring the James River; on their return, work began on more substantial fortifications. By mid-June Jamestown boasted a triangular fort of upright logs, with "three Bulwarkes at every corner like a halfe moone, and foure or five pieces of Artillerie mounted in them." During the sweltering summer, when disease and famine hit hardest, the few healthy men kept constant watch lest a concerted attack or silent infiltration bring a sudden end to the colony. Englishmen who wandered outside the fort risked injury or death at the hands of lurking Indians. The toll mounted.

On the whole, however, the trend of Indian-white relations appeared favorable. On June 14, a week before Newport's departure for England, several Indians came to Jamestown to explain that the recent attack on the fort had been perpetrated by minor tribes subservient to the great chief Powhatan; the friendly natives offered to help the English fight their enemies or make peace with them. They also warned the settlers to cut the weeds near the fort to reduce the danger of ambushes — advice that should have been unnecessary to a military man like Captain Smith. And in September, without supplication on the part of the colonists, several Indians arrived bearing corn. Though half ripe, it was a godsend to hungry men. This timely display of cordiality seemed to further vindicate Newport's conciliatory policy. For the moment all went well between Indians and whites. "But," noted John Smith, "our comaedies never endured long without a Tragedie." And in the colony's next tragedy, he played the central role.

After Newport's departure for England in the summer of 1607, John Smith became the principal negotiator with the Indians and leader of expeditions into the interior. In December he led a party up the Chickahominy River, a branch of the James that turned northwest about six miles above Jamestown. Taking a barge and a small contingent, Smith pushed up river as far as the vessel could go, then left seven men behind while he continued by canoe with two companions and two Indian guides. Disaster struck when the men on the barge disobeyed his instructions and went ashore; they were attacked and slaughtered. Other Indians ambushed Smith when he went fowling, and slew the guards he left with the canoe. Smith put up a stiff fight and killed two of his assailants before slipping into a quagmire. Waist-deep in muck and armed only with an empty pistol, he finally surrendered.

For the next several weeks Smith was once more a helpless prisoner. The events of his captivity are known only from his own writings or those of friends who reported what they heard from him, and it may be, as Smith's critics have contended, that he fabricated much of his story. But distorted or not, the episode would be crucial to Smith and to the Jamestown colony.

Smith displayed once again the bravery that had marked his earlier career. He showed no fear of Indians, either individually or collectively, any more than he had for Turbashaw, Bonny Mulgro, or the armies of Islam. Before his capture by the Indians he had singlehandedly held off two hundred armed warriors (according to his account) ; thereafter he so impressed his captors with his courage and skill (again by his account) that in the end he gained not only his freedom but their high regard. Yet Smith had no strong affection for the American natives. Throughout his dealings with them the captain treated Indians like common adversaries, grudgingly giving them credit for strength or wisdom, but never trusting or cherishing them.

The Indians, in turn, considered Smith their principal enemy. They tried to kill him before his capture, and might have succeeded had he not used his guide for a shield. And they undoubtedly considered executing him in accordance with tribal customs — Smith later learned that one of his men had perished in a gruesome torture ceremony. But partly because Smith was a captain, and therefore a prize worth holding for ransom, and partly because he dazzled his captors with a pocket compass, they spared him for disposition by Powhatan. In the meantime he received kind treatment, and an abundance of venison and corn bread, while the Indians interrogated him about the English settlement. Smith put up a good bluff, exaggerating the strength of the English and predicting destruction of the Indians if they should harm him. The ruse worked. His captors not only spared his life but saved him from assassination by the father of an Indian he had shot before his capture. Smith now became a showpiece as the Indians took him from town to town and eventually to the great chief Powhatan.

Powhatan impressed Smith, as he impressed all Englishmen, as a proud and majestic figure. That did not deter Smith from lying flagrantly about English intentions. "Hee asked mee the cause of our comming," recalled Smith. "I tolde him being in fight with the Spaniards our enemie, beeing over powred, neare put to retreat, and by exteame weather put to this shore . . . [and] our Pinn[a]sse being leake wee were inforced to stay to mend her, till Captaine Newport my father came to conduct us away." When Powhatan wanted to know why the English explored so far inland, Smith insisted that they intended to attack the Monocans, Powhatan's enemies to the west, for killing a child of Newport. That appealed to the chief; he regaled Smith with stories of his own domain and lands to the west, and invited the captain "to live with him upon his River," to engage in trade, "and none should disturbe us." "This request I promised to performe," Smith admitted, with no real intention of doing so — at least not in the sense the Indian meant. Powhatan released the Englishman and sent him back to Jamestown.

So reads Smith's initial version of his release, published as part of his "True Relation" of recent events in Virginia. He wrote it in early June of 1608 and sent it on *Phoenix* to England where it was printed later that year. It may originally have mentioned the intercession of Pocahontas and other events of his captivity that appeared only in his later writings, but the "True Relation" fell into the hands of an editor who deleted the parts he considered too personal or too detrimental to the reputation of the colony. In any event, the version published in 1608 mentioned no rescue by the Indian princess. Nor did Smith's *Map of Virginia* (1612), which told of his captivity in two sentences: "A month those Barbarians kept him prisoner. Many strange triumphes and conjurations they made of him: yet hee so demeaned himselfe amongst them, as he not only diverted them from surprising the Fort; but procure his owne liberty, and got himself and his company such estimation amongst them, that those Salvages admired him as a demi-God." This account showed Smith at his vainest; no room here for rescue by an adolescent girl.

The episode took on a far different appearance in 1624 when Captain Smith produced his *Generall Historie* of British America. Although Pocahontas had died several years earlier, she had become a legend: the savage princess who converted to Christianity, married an Englishman, visited England and met the royal family. There was no need then to suppress the story of her aid. Critics of Smith have seen the matter less generously: with Pocahontas and Powhatan dead, no restraints prevented the captain from inventing an attractive anecdote. Who could deny Smith's claim that when the Indians had been "ready with their clubs, to beate out his braines, *Pocahontas* the Kings dearest daughter, when no intreaty could prevaile, got his head in her armes, and laid her owne upon his to save him from death: whereat the Emperour was contented he should live. . . ."? The truth lies buried with the captain and his Indian captors.

Whether through Pocahontas' intercession or his own negotiations with Powhatan, early in 1608 Smith returned, accompanied by four Indian guides, to the English outpost at Jamestown. His reception there fell short of his expectations. On the Levitical grounds that he had been responsible for the death of two of his men, and hence should lose his own life, the council sentenced him to the gallows. Only Smith's blunt refusal to submit to the hangman, and Newport's timely return from England, rescued him once again from an ignominious death at the hands of his own countrymen.

With that event Smith's American career reached its perigee. Thereafter his influence grew as that of Wingfield, Ratcliffe, and Martin declined. Back in June Smith had gained his rightful seat on the governing council through the intercession of Newport and Reverend Hunt, but since then his sole assignments had been to map the area and barter with the Indians. Now, gradually and grudgingly, the colony recognized Smith's considerable talents, especially in contrast to his fellow councillors'.

President Wingfield proved no leader. He rapidly lost the confidence of his followers by keeping for himself and his cronies the colony's precious supply of sack and *aqua vitae,* at least the three surviving councillors — Ratcliffe, Smith, and Martin — were sufficiently convinced of it to oust Wingfield from command less than six months after his installation. John Ratcliffe, elected to succeed him, also showed little skill at solving the colony's problems. Some new members joined the council in January 1608 when Captain Newport arrived with the "first supply," but as unseasoned colonists they played a relatively passive role. As the need for firm leadership became more apparent, both in dealings with the natives and in controlling the settlers, the colony increasingly turned to Smith. In September 1608 Ratcliffe's term as president, limited by charter to one year, expired. In the ensuing election Smith won the office, "which till then," the captain later insisted, "by no means would he accept, though he was often importuned thereunto." Reluctant candidate or not, Smith now had charge of England's only American outpost; its survival would depend in large part on his judgment and strength of will.

C.Smith taketh the King of Pamavukee prisoner 1608

Smith seizes Opechancanough by the hair,
while English and Indian armies fight in the background.

III

President Smith

From the second week in September 1608, through the following August, John Smith ruled the colony almost singlehandedly. According to the royal charter he was bound by the advice of his councillors, but their rapid demise — through departure or death — removed that curb. He was bound too by instructions from the London Company, but the colony's needs and the slowness of transatlantic communications left him free to improvise. That did not mean he had everything his own way: neither company nor Indians nor settlers bent cheerfully to the captain's will. His accomplishments came hard; he succeeded only because of his rare blend of common sense and tenacity. Virginia needed both.

No sooner had Smith taken office than Christopher Newport sailed into Jamestown with the "second supply." That should have boded well for Smith and the colony. Newport had earlier given him timely support, and the colony was in dire need of almost everything — food, weapons, tools, clothing, and trading goods. Instead, Newport brought a hodgepodge of irrelevant supplies and seventy more mouths to feed. He also brought new instructions that pushed Smith's temper to the boiling point.

The company had ordered Newport to remain in America until one or more items were discovered: gold, a route to the South Sea, or survivors of the Roanoke colony. To help accomplish these fanciful tasks, the company sent a gold refiner, a five-section barge, and a plethora of gentlemen. Smith scoffed at the whole scheme, especially the barge, which the company expected Newport to carry across the mountains from the eastern fall line to an equivalent point on a westward-flowing river. "If he had burnt her to ashes," Smith snorted, "one might have carried her in a bag, but as she is, five hundred cannot." In the margin of his later account of this period, Smith summed up his scorn for the London Company's impractical instructions: "No better way to overthrow the business then by our instructors."

Adding to the colony's woes was the odd assortment of new recruits. They were not the blacksmiths and carpenters and "diggers up of trees" that Smith needed; instead he got twenty-eight gentlemen, fourteen artisans of the wrong kinds, only twelve laborers, two boys, and two women — the colony's first. Smith did not complain about the women; he considered family life essential to permanent colonization. But he wanted men who were inured to hard work, who had appropriate skills, and whose commitment to the colony went further than their own selfish concerns. On that score the second supply was as deficient as the original expedition. Even several skilled Germans and Poles, sent to make tar, glass, and potash, did not impress the president. There was no time for such projects when his men suffered acutely from hunger, exposure, and Indian attacks. The company gave top priority to the adventurers' profits. Smith had to keep the settlers alive.

Newport remained in Virginia through the fall of 1608. To his dismay — but in fulfillment of Smith's predictions — he accomplished none of his goals. An excursion to the west, for which Newport commandeered 120 of the best men (from a total population of 200), found neither the South Sea nor precious metals, even though its refiner thought he discovered silver ore. Subsequent expeditions failed to locate the Roanoke survivors. The only information gleaned from the distant Indians confirmed what Powhatan had insisted from the outset: there were no survivors.

PRESIDENT SMITH   43

Newport fared almost as poorly in his attempt to implement another of the company's plans. He had been directed to conduct an elaborate coronation of Powhatan, replete with gifts, pageantry, and a copper crown. Because the company's records for the early years have not survived, its intentions remain obscure; presumably it wanted symbolic acknowledgment from Powhatan that he was subject to the English crown. That would not give the English title to his lands, but it would justify action in the King's name when disputes over boundaries, treaties, trade, or jurisprudence occurred. Accordingly, the company instructed Newport to crown Powhatan as a sign of the chief's authority over the Indians of the area (which obviously he already had), and of his subservience to James I of England (which obviously he would not willingly yield).

The event turned out to be a minor farce and revealed the differences in English and Indian perspectives. The Indian monarch refused to go to Jamestown for the ceremony. He too was a king, Powhatan declared; let the English, if they wished to give him presents, come to his village. In the end they did. With whatever pomp and ceremony they could muster in the Virginia forest, the Englishmen presented Powhatan with a basin and ewer, bed and other furniture, and a scarlet cloak. "But a foule trouble there was," Smith reported, "to make him kneele to receive his Crowne, he neither knowing the majesty nor meaning of a Crowne, nor bending of the knee . . . ; at last by leaning hard on his shoulders he a little stooped, and three having the crowne in their hands put it on his head. . . ." Chief Powhatan returned the dubious honor in his own fashion by giving his mantle and old shoes to Captain Newport.

Smith knew that Powhatan's coronation meant little to the chief and would strengthen Indian-English relations only as long as Powhatan saw in it some tangible benefits. Rather, Smith believed, it had done more harm than good. Powhatan had been very cooperative of late, "till this stately kind of soliciting, made him so much overvalue himselfe, that he respected us as much as nothing at all." Newport would soon depart, leaving Smith to cope with Powhatan's swollen ego.

Before he sailed, Newport made a few more attempts to win over the Indians. Powhatan had already given permission to the English to settle in his territory on two conditions—"to be loving to his people, and to defend him from his enemies. . . ." To accomplish the second provision, Newport offered to lead an expedition against the Monacans to the west. Powhatan was not fooled by the offer; he rightly suspected that Newport's interest in an inland foray stemmed more from a desire to search for gold and routes to the South Sea than to "Terrify & kill his Adversaryes." Powhatan also feared that the English might make an alliance with his enemies; he accordingly refused to provide guides and carriers and allowed only Namontack, who had spent the previous year in England and was now the principal interpreter, to go along. And it is more than likely that Powhatan would have denied even that assistance had he not wanted to have a spy in the Englishmen's camp. He need not have worried. Newport visited only two Monacan villages, made neither peace nor war, and returned to Jamestown empty-handed.

To meet Powhatan's other condition — making the English "loving" to the natives — Newport tried hard to show them respect and do them justice. Insisting that while he remained in Virginia his special instructions superseded the president's authority on Indian affairs, he strove to curb what he considered Smith's maltreatment of the natives. Newport refused to use strong-arm tactics to get Indian corn, and in one instance he had an Englishman, alleged to have pushed an Indian, bound to a tree and beaten with a cudgel. To Smith's way of thinking, Captain Newport's sole contribution was to make food harder to get. Before Newport arrived "we had the Salvages in that *decorum* . . . that we feared not to get victuals for 500." By the time he left, the Indians were again holding back, and prices had soared. Newport's sailors had exploited the hunger and indolence of the settlers by trading them ship's food for furs; to get the pelts, unscrupulous colonists bartered everything in sight that appealed to the Indians — axes, hoes, chisels, pikeheads, even powder and shot.

Smith's sigh of relief must have echoed through the streets of Jamestown when Newport finally weighed anchor in December 1608. Instead of gold he carried clapboard and wainscoating, cut by Smith and the others who toiled while Newport had chased his rainbows, as well as preliminary samples of tar, pitch, glass, and other local products. He carried too a blistering letter from President Smith to the London Company. "My rude Answere," Smith called it, and in an era of strict social proprieties, it was.

It was also a remarkably forthright and perceptive statement on the realities of colonization. "Though I be no scholer, I am past a schoole-boy," he reminded the company. He had kept London well-informed about the true state of the colony, yet it obstinately acted on less knowledgeable advice (Newport's in particular) to the detriment of all concerned. Smith chided the company too for its ridiculous instructions to Newport — they had been pointless and costly. Finally, Smith lectured his superiors on Virginia's economic prospects. It was foolhardy to expect cargoes of lumber and other goods, such as Russia and Sweden supplied, from an outpost "of ignorant miserable soules, that are scarce able to get wherewith to live, and defend our selves against the inconstant *Salvages:* finding but here and there a tree fit for the purpose, and want all things els the Russians have." He needed good men, adequate draft animals, and a free hand with the Indians. For the foreseeable future he would also need food from England. "Though there be fish in the Sea, fowles in the ayre, Beast in the woods, their bounds are so large, they so wilde, and we so weake and ignorant, we cannot much trouble them." "These are the causes," Smith concluded, "that have kept us in

Virginia, from laying such a foundation, that ere this might have given much better content and satisfaction; . . . as yet you must not looke for any profitable returnes."

After Newport left, Smith resumed his own brand of Indian diplomacy. Its cornerstones were to instill fear (Smith would have used a more euphemistic term) and to avoid open warfare. The former ensured adequate supplies of corn and free movement by Englishmen through the countryside. The latter saved lives, on both sides, and kept the Indians from moving westward where Smith could no longer barter with them for food and other goods. The Indians can plant crops anywhere, one of them warned him, but the colony cannot survive without their harvests; "if you proceed in revenge, we will abandon the Country." During his year in office Smith avoided all-out force, and the Indians, except Powhatan, did not move away.

In terms of the colony's needs, Smith's policy worked well: he seemed always to get corn where others failed. And he accorded the natives some mercy and justice. But Smith cajoled or bullied to get what he wanted, and often he provoked incidents that led to bloodshed. If the colony needed food, and the Indians because of a poor harvest had little, Smith fumed and ranted, pretending far more anger than he felt, until he had his way. Often he paid for what he took, somehow satisfying his own conscience that the score had been settled. Nor did he limit such imperious tactics to gathering food. On a scouting party in the winter of 1608–1609, Smith and twelve Englishmen rested for a few days in the village of Kiskiack; "to suppresse the insolencie of those proud Salvages," Smith forced the Indians to provide shelter and guards and to "give us what wee wanted." They dared not retaliate.

There were, however, several fatal skirmishes. Despite Smith's intention to preserve the colony without shedding blood, his publications tell a disturbing story. In the six months following Newport's departure, about a dozen Indians were killed by the colonists, many more were wounded, several were incarcerated in the Jamestown jail, and one Smith "not only beate, but spurned him like a dogge." Smith also burned houses and confiscated canoes and fishing weirs. Occasional force was the only way, he contended, to deal with "such a dailey daring trecherous people." To his critics he pointed out how gentle he was by comparison to the Spanish conquistadors. And to those who sat comfortably in England and reprimanded him for maltreating the Indians Smith retorted, "I could wish those [were] here, that make those [Indians] seeme Saints, and me an oppressor." He even tried to get Newport to spend a full year in Virginia so he could see the fruits of his indulgent policy. There is no denying, however, that Smith was often arrogant and occasionally brutal; the best that can be said is that in an era of low regard for human suffering he was less callous than most of his contemporaries.

Smith had tactics to lessen the probability of bloodshed. One of his settlers described the captain's modus operandi: "To express all our quarrels, trecheries and incounters amongst those Salvages, I should be too tedious: but in brcefe, at all times we so incountered them, and curbed their insolencies, that they concluded with presents to purchase peace; yet we lost not a man: at our first meeting, our Captaine ever observed this order, to demand their bowes and arrowes, swordes, mantells and furrs, with some childe or two for hostage, whereby we could quickly perceive, when they intended any villany." Stripped of their arms, and with their children in English hands, the Indians seldom risked "villany," justified or not.

They did, however, try to take Smith unawares. That failed too, for the captain had, it seemed, a sixth sense to warn him of ambushes. He also continued his inordinate luck in single combat. When the Chief of Paspahegh tried to shoot Smith, alone and armed only with a short sword, "the President prevented his shoot by grapling with him, and the Salvage as well prevented him from drawing his faucheon, and perforce bore him to the River to have drowned him. Long they struggled in the water, till the President got such a hold on his throat, he had near strangled the King; but having drawne his faucheon to cut off his head, seeing how pittifully he begged his life, he led him prisoner to *James* Towne, and put him in chaynes."

Threats often served as effectively as violence. "For your sake onely," he told Powhatan, "we have curbed our thirsting desire of revenge"; otherwise the Indians would see "the crueltie we use to our enemies. . . ." Powhatan opted for peace. So did his subordinate chiefs. When Opechancanough, leader of the Pamunkey tribe and a half-brother of Powhatan, surrounded a party of Englishmen and appeared ready to slaughter them, Smith challenged him to individual combat. "My body shall bee as naked as yours," Smith promised; "the Isle in your river is a fit place . . . and the conquerour (of us two) shall be Lord and Master over all our men." Opechancanough, perhaps remembering the three Turks' heads on Smith's shield, declined. But the captain was not finished with this adversary. Seizing him by the hair, Smith shoved a pistol against his breast, and paraded him amongst his astonished warriors. Smith kept his grip until he had delivered another threatening harangue: "If you shoot but one Arrow to shed one drop of bloud of any of my men, or steale the least of these Beads, or Copper . . . I will not cease revenge (if once I begin) so long as I can heare where to finde one of your Nation. . . ." Smith professed peace, but he wanted food even more. "You promised to fraught my Ship [with corn] ere I departed," he bellowed, "and so you shall; or I meane to load her with your dead carcasses. . . ." Such tactics got supplies for the colony, and they may have prevented wholesale carnage. They did not promote racial harmony.

Somewhat offsetting Smith's militant approach to chiefs and tribesmen was his affection for Pocahontas. Whatever her role in gaining his release from captivity, the Indian girl sincerely liked the grizzled soldier and frequently visited him at Jamestown. She must also have been intrigued by the strange sights that could be seen only at the English outpost: framed houses and huge ships; peculiar animals — horses, cattle, sheep, hogs, and dogs much larger and more ferocious than the native breed. There were fascinating gadgets too — compasses and mirrors, firearms and steel-bladed knives, axes and iron kettles. And the people — covered from head to foot in woven cloth, with bearded faces, odd hair styles, and an unintelligible language that could be recorded on sheets of parchment and bound into leather-covered volumes. Curiosity worked both ways of course. The colonists now had a native visitor who posed no threat and sought no trade. "A well featured but wanton young girle," recalled William Strachey, who arrived in Virginia soon after Smith left, ". . . sometymes resorting to our Fort, of the age then of 11. or 12. yeares, [she would] gett the boyes forth with her into the markett place and make them wheele, falling on their handes turning their heeles upwardes, whome she would follow, and wheel so her self naked as she was all the Fort over. . . ." Strachey used "wanton" in the sense of "frolicsome"; her fascination with John Smith was that of a preadolescent girl for an older and awesome man.

More important to the colony than her crush on the captain was her willingness, even eagerness, to warn him of danger from her own father. All accounts portray her as Powhatan's favorite daughter, yet on several occasions she risked her life to reveal his plots. In fact, Pocahontas' last meeting with Smith in Virginia took place in Powhatan's village where Smith had gone to parley with the chief; "in that dark night [she] came through the irksome woods, and told our Captaine great cheare should be sent us by and by: but *Powhatan* . . . would after come kill us all. . . ." Smith tried to thank Pocahontas with gifts, "but with teares running downe her cheekes, she said she durst not be seen to have any: for if *Powhatan* should know it, she were but dead, and so shee ranne away by herselfe as she came." The colony's survival, and Smith's, owed almost as much to Pocahontas' friendship as to the president's courage.

Throughout his stay in Virginia, John Smith and Powhatan jostled for power. They had grudging admiration for each other, and at times exhibited a superficial cordiality. But each considered the other his prime adversary, to be destroyed if necessary. On several occasions, according to the English sources, Powhatan tried to kill Smith by poison, ambush, or sorcery. Smith, for his part, more than once advocated a preventive attack on the chief's stronghold. Eventually Smith gave up those plans when Powhatan moved his seat of government to a village further inland. Still, fairly amicable trade continued between English and Indians while each leader kept a wary eye on the other. Powhatan was apparently willing to part with some of his corn for English tools and trinkets, so long as the English did not attack his people. Smith was willing to barter almost anything for food.

The exception was firearms. In case of war with the Indians, Smith counted on pistols and muskets to offset his opponent's overwhelming numerical advantage. "If you dare stand but to discharge your pieces," Smith assured his men, "the very smoake will bee sufficient to affright them." Now and then the Indians got a gun by illicit purchase or theft or from a slain colonist. Without understanding their use and repair, however, the Indians gained little. In one instance, several Indians who acquired a bag of gunpowder lost their lives by mishandling it; others tried to raise powder by planting it in the ground. In any event, Smith made sure they had no guns in which to use it. Once when Smith was away from Jamestown, Powhatan acquired a sizable arsenal of English weapons by sending two Germans, assigned to build him an English-style house, to Jamestown with a request for arms that purported to be from the president. The trick worked, but Smith eventually regained most of the weapons by his usual strong-arm methods. Similarly, he made clear that stealing English firearms would lead to drastic reprisal. When a Chickahominy stole a pistol, Smith seized two tribesmen "knowne to be his confederates," threw one in a dungeon and threatened to hang him if the other did not return the gun in twelve hours. It was in Smith's hands long before the deadline.

That incident had a sequel in keeping with Smith's penchant for turning unpropitious situations to his advantage. Purely by accident the Indian in the dungeon almost died from smoke inhalation. The Chickahominies thought their tribesman dead; Smith knew better but seized the opportunity to add superstition to his arsenal of controls over the Indians by promising to restore the victim to life in return for peace with the tribe. He then revived the captive, whose dazed condition convinced the Indians that Smith still held him entranced. The captain gained further concessions from the tribe before his prisoner recovered completely. News of Smith's supernatural power spread rapidly, and soon Powhatan as well as the Chickahominies did whatever President Smith ordered. They returned tools (including some the English had not missed), sent food and skins, and delivered all Indians who stole from the colonists to Jamestown for punishment. Smith, of course, felt no compunction against bamboozling the Indians into such cooperation.

Through it all, Powhatan felt powerless to resist. "Captain Smith," he protested, "you insist on having whatsoever you demand." And so he did, to the short-run benefit of the colony and the perturbation of the Indians. "All the countrie," marvelled a settler, "became absolutely as free for us, as for themselves." That happy situation would not survive the captain's departure from Virginia, however. Rightly or wrongly, Smith had not made the Indians "subject to the English," as he claimed, but to himself. A few years after Smith returned to England a settler reported that "the Salvages no sooner understood of Captaine *Smiths* losse, but they all revolted, and did murder and spoil all they could incounter."

Several colonists, whose collective account of the period Smith later incorporated into his history of Virginia, attested to his achievements as president. In the spring of 1609, they reported, the colony made remarkable progress in manufacturing, agriculture, and the rebuilding of the village. The pitch, tar, soap ash, and glass works moved ahead, as did the weaving of fishing weirs and nets. Smith's men constructed a blockhouse on the neck of land connecting Jamestown to the mainland where a garrison let no one "passe or repasse, Salvage nor Christian, without the Presidents order." Other workers built houses, reroofed the church and storehouse, and dug a well of "excellent sweete water." Thirty to forty acres were "digged and planted," while two Indian prisoners gave directions for sowing maize. A new blockhouse on Hog Island, a few miles downstream from Jamestown, warned of approaching vessels.

For the moment all seemed well in Virginia. Then Smith discovered that rats had infested the casks of corn with which the settlers, still numbering close to two hundred, had expected to survive until the fall harvest. For a time the Indians provided enough game to ward off starvation. When the situation became critical, Smith dispersed the colony, sending twenty men under George Percy to Point Comfort to fish and as many to the falls, and another seventy or eighty downriver to live on oysters. Some even moved into native villages, safe in the knowledge that "wee had such a commanding power at *James* towne they durst not wrong us of a pin."

As the colonists grew weaker from inadequate diet, and as discouragement and hot weather set in, Smith faced a perennial problem in early Jamestown: many settlers simply would not make intelligent and energetic efforts to survive. There was plenty of sturgeon, which could be dried, mixed with caviar, sorell, and "other wholesome hearbes" for bread; so too could the roots of some native plants. Supplemented by game and berries the thirty to forty industrious settlers "lived very well, in regard of such a diet." Smith had to force the remaining one hundred and fifty Englishmen to gather their own food. They preferred to trade whatever they owned — gems included — to the Indians rather than expend any energy. The idlers, in turn, resented Smith's stringent policies and some began to plot escape to Newfoundland in the colony's pinnace. With characteristic vigor, Smith punished the ringleader, "a most crafty fellow," and gave a no-nonsense speech to the rest. He assured the settlers that he would have corn from the Indians if there were any to get. He also threatened the gallows to any "runners for Newfoundland," and to those too lazy to work Smith promised "to force you from your Idlenesse, and punish you if you rayle." Each man must gather daily as much food as the president did, or "be banished from the Fort as a drone till he amend his conditions or starve." Some muttered at Smith's strictness, but of the two hundred men only about eighteen died during his administration, eleven of them by drowning when they went foraging in violation of the president's orders.

Among the victims of that accident were Matthew Scrivener and Richard Waldo, members of the council. Earlier Smith had sent home with Captain Newport another councillor and perpetual troublemaker, John Ratcliffe (who for reasons obscure to Smith and everyone since had changed his name to Sicklemore), "least the company [here] should cut his throat." That left Captain Peter Winne as the sole councillor other than the president, but Winne died, probably of disease, in early 1609. From then until the following September Smith ruled alone, to the dismay of the less orderly settlers. "There are now no Counsellers to protect you, nor curbe my endevors," he reminded them; "therefore he that offendeth, let him assuredly expect his due punishment." Smith was now judge, jury, and — if he chose to be — executioner. He did not, however, have to go that far. Because everyone knew that the president meant what he said, all hands labored hard enough to avoid his wrath. He had other ways of encouraging them too. He set an admirable example himself, toiling as hard as any man, and harder than most. He also let public opinion exert its subtle pressure by posting lists of the industrious and the laggards "to incourage the good, and with shame to spurre on the rest. . . ." And Smith did not set demands higher than he had a right to expect. He asked only six hours of work per day; the remainder could be spent "in Pastime and merry exercises."

A basic problem for Smith, as for the officers who preceded and followed him, lay in the nature of the settlers themselves. Few arrived in Virginia with any thought of staying; most expected a far softer life than they found; and almost all resented chores that did not coincide with the social status or occupational specialty they had enjoyed back home. Gentlemen refused manual labor; artisans objected to unskilled tasks; soldiers resisted civilian work of any kind. Smith somehow managed — partly by example, partly by threat — to keep the colonists alive. But even he could not prevent dissention. For a time he faced treason by the Germans and a Swiss ("those damned *Dutch*-men," Smith fumed) ; they urged Powhatan to crush the colony and supplied him with guns and ammunition. Smith also faced persistent factionalism among the English settlers, even among the leaders. Ratcliffe was merely the most flagrant example, and unfortunately a recurring one. Smith warned the London Company that "If he and *Archer* returne againe, they are sufficient to keepe us always in factions." Both were soon back in Virginia, but, fortunately for Smith, not until his term had almost expired.

Smith's principal solution to both indolence and dissent was military discipline. He divided the entire colony into units of ten or fifteen as their tasks required, established a rotating watch, and indoctrinated the able bodied in military drill. Each Saturday the president mustered his men in a clearing — appropriately called Smithfield — near the fort where he taught them how to march and maneuver, and how to handle a musket. While his marksmen blasted away at trees, "sometimes more than an hundred Salvages would stand in amasement." That too was part of Smith's modus operandi: he wanted the Indians to see the destructive power of English firearms. He also wanted them to know that the settlers were healthy and under vigorous leadership.

Although President Smith kept the outpost at Jamestown freer from illness, indolence, and attack than at any time since its founding, the company in England did not rejoice. In July 1609, Captain Samuel Argall arrived at Jamestown "with letters that much taxed our President for his hard dealing with the Salvages" and for failing to load the ships with marketable commodities. Smith sent word back to London that he could not "returne that wealth they expected, or observe the[i]re instructions to indure the Salvages insolencies," without better men and more supplies.

Both were on the way. While Smith read the disturbing letters brought by Argall, a fleet of nine ships headed toward Virginia. On board were almost five hundred settlers, including many women and children; also a new governor, Sir Thomas Gates, and several other recently appointed officials. With the first ships of the third supply, which limped into the James on 11 August after a stormy voyage, a new era in Virginia history began. One mark of that era was the closing of John Smith's direct contribution to the English conquest of America.

A modern impression of Jamestown during "the starving time"

I V
Time of Troubles

THE LONDON COMPANY expected to earn at least modest profits within two years. Instead it reaped nothing but ill reports and empty hulls. Accordingly, the principal promoters of British America decided to make some basic changes in the structure of both the London Company and its colony. In the spring of 1609 they launched still another effort to find a workable formula for New World colonization.

Some problems stemmed from the royal charter of 1606, which had been too restrictive. Because the colonists had discovered no precious metals or rivers to the South Sea, the area to be explored and exploited needed enlarging; because expenses had vastly outgrown predictions and no returns had come from the colony, new opportunities for raising funds had to be created; and because prospective stockholders faced uncertain dividends, long-term investments had to be encouraged. Early in 1609, "at the humble suite and request of sondrie our lovinge and well disposed subjects," King James issued a new charter that incorporated "The Tresorer and Companie of Adventurers and Planters of the Citty of London for the Firste Collonie in Virginia." Among the patentees were some of England's most distinguished names, countless lesser gentry, scores of companies of craftsmen — among them the fishmongers, vintners, pewterers, wax-chandlers, embroiderers, and musicians — as well as clergymen, merchants, and toward the end of the list, Captain John Smith. Sir Thomas Smythe received appointment as treasurer, the principal officer of the organization; he would be aided by a council numbering more than fifty, including the Lord Mayor of London, the Earl of Southampton, Lord de la Warr, the Bishop of Bath and Wells, Sir Francis Bacon, Sir Edwin Sandys, and Sir Thomas Gates. Although the King made the initial appointments, replacements were to be made by a majority vote of the assembled members of the corporation; each new councillor must be a stockholder and take an oath to the Crown. The council would exercise full authority over the colony. Guided by self-interest as well as public zeal, the management in London would, presumably, bring speedy improvement to the Virginia venture.

Armed with its new prerogatives, the London Company immediately began to reorganize the colony's government. In lieu of the president and resident council, always bickering and without sufficient authority, the company substituted a governor of its own appointment. He would be assisted by subordinate officials and an advisory council. The governorship went to Sir Thomas Gates, a veteran of Drake's American expedition of 1585 and of warfare in the Low Countries. Gates' advisory council, named in the detailed instructions from the company, included Sir George Somers, newly designated Admiral of Virginia; Captain John Smith, "nowe President"; Captains John Ratcliffe, Peter Winne, John Martin, Richard Waldo, Thomas Wood, Edward Fleetwood, and Matthew Scrivener. In a fitting conjunction of a name and a job, Scrivener was appointed the council's secretary. The company, of course, did not know that he, Waldo, and Winne were dead.

Gates' instructions directed him to sail for Virginia "with the first winde," commanding six hundred men in a fleet of eight ships and a pinnace. Specific directions on what to do after his arrival in Virginia reflected the company's view of what had gone wrong during the colony's first two years. His "principall order and Care" was to protect true religion; that required preaching and the administration of the sacraments "accordinge to the constitucions of the Church of England in all fundamentall pointes." Most of the remainder of the twenty-three sections of the instructions dealt with the more mundane matters John Smith thought he had handled brilliantly, and the company thought he had conducted miserably — relations with the Indians.

The company had long accused the colony of treating the natives too roughly; rather than browbeat them for corn, the colonists should have introduced the Indians to the glories of Christianity and the benefits of English civilization. That could best be done, the company advised, by taking "some convenient nomber of their Children to be brought up in your language, and manners." If the governor found it convenient, he should also "remove from them their Quiocasockcs or Priestes by a surprise of them all and detayninge them prisoners. . . ." This strategy made perfect sense to devout Christians, of course: the Indian priests beguiled and terrified their subjects so that "while they live amounge them to poyson and infecte them their mindes, you shall never make any great progres into this glorious worke, nor have any Civill peace or concurre with them." That, in turn, justified more drastic measures. "In case of necessity or conveniency," the company informed Gates, "we pronounce it not crueltie nor breache of Charity to deale more sharpely with them and to proceede even to dache [death] with these murtherers of Soules. . . ." In short, Gates' instructions were to be kind to the Indians, convert and educate them, but first eliminate their priests, by fair means or foul. The distinction between Smith's threats while taking what he wanted, and the company's superficial kindness while exterminating their religious leaders, was likely to be lost on the Indians. No native sources have survived to show what the Indians thought about either Smith or the company. Very likely they concluded that the only good Englishman was a dead Englishman.

The company told Gates how to deal, just as insidiously,

with chiefs. Powhatan, the company admitted, "loved not our neighborhood and therefore you may no way trust him." The solution: "if you finde it not best to make him your prisoner yet you must make him your tributary, and all other his werowances [subordinate chiefs] about him shall first to acknowledge no other Lord but King James." Freed from Powhatan's control the petty chiefs would bring much needed provisions into the colony; they must pay the English for freeing them from Powhatan's tyranny and for protecting them from other enemies. Such tribute in annual payments of corn, dye, and skins, and in labor, would not only provide desired commodities but would also "be a meanes of Clearinge much ground of wood and of reducing them to laboure and trade. . . . " Should the Indians flee into the country on the approach of the English, Gates was to seize their chiefs and all known successors. By training their future leaders in English manners and religion and installing them as the heads of tribes, "their people will easily obey you and become in time Civill and Christian."

Unfortunately, admitted the company, fear of the English and a surfeit of copper made trade with the nearby tribes unlikely. Better to make friends with distant Indians, hostile to those near Jamestown, who would appreciate copper more, would be less likely to make trouble, and would be eager to trade. Especially recommended were several tribes in enmity with Powhatan: "with those you may hold trade and freindeship good Cheape." And wherever possible, the company suggested, make the Indians bring their goods to English forts by pretending not to need their products; this would save the English precious time otherwise wasted in seeking trade at Indian villages. The Indians, however, must not be allowed to use their visits to the settlements to learn any crafts related to the manufacture or repair of weapons.

Matters other than Indian relations received the company's attention. Because the colony had often been laxly run under the first charter, there would now be (in the words of a com-

pany tract) "one *able* and *absolute Governor.*" The company
directed Gates to use martial law when necessary and to
administer justice "rather uppon the naturall right and equity
then uppon the nicenes and lettre of the lawe which per-
plexeth in this tender body. . . ." Here was a frank admission
that traditional English liberties must be curtailed in
America. The New World needed new tactics, in this case "a
Summary and arbitrary way of Justice discreetely mingled
with those gravities and fourmes of magistracy as shall in your
discrecion seeme aptest for you and that place. . . ." The
company also wanted a new seat of government in the colony.
Jamestown had proved "unwholsome and but in the Marish of
Virginia." Gates should seek a sunny, dry, cleared, and well-
protected location, retaining Jamestown only as a port. Two
other plantations should be established, one at the falls of the
James River, the other at an Indian site near Roanoke, where
they would find "a brave and fruiteful seat." A fort at Point
Comfort would protect the settlements from external and
internal enemies; Indians were forbidden to dwell between
the English and the sea lest they become guides for attacking
forces. The company recommended John Smith for the chore
of clearing natives from the coastal area.

Armed with these elaborate instructions and a copy of the
new charter, Sir Thomas Gates boarded *Sea Venture* in mid-
May 1609. Fellow passengers included Sir George Somers, who
had replaced Christopher Newport in command of the London Company's naval operations. Newport, now vice-admiral,
commanded *Sea Venture,* flagship of this latest and largest
English colonizing expedition. Delays kept the fleet coast-
bound for several weeks; not until early June did it leave sight
of England. Disease soon struck; on two ships alone, thirty-two
bodies had to be thrown overboard. Then on the 25th of July
a violent storm scattered the fleet as it passed near the West
Indies. A small catch perished with all hands. Seven of the
remaining ships survived, battered but afloat, and eventually

reached Jamestown. But the flagship, with all the principal leaders, the charter, and the company's instructions, caught the full brunt of the storm. For three days and nights the crew bailed frantically to keep the ship from foundering, while some of the passengers found solace in prayer and others sought relief in the bottle. At last the raging ocean cast *Sea Venture* against the coast of Bermuda where it miraculously wedged itself between two rocks. The wind abated, "and with extreme joy, even almost to amazednesse" all hands took to the small boats and made their way safely to shore. They even salvaged most of the cargo.

Too late the folly of letting all of the expedition's leaders billet in the same ship became obvious. One hundred miles from Virginia and shunned by ships of all nations ("it hath beene to the *Spaniards* more fearefull then an Utopian Purgatory," Smith reported) , Bermuda seemed likely to become the graveyard of all one hundred fifty seamen and prospective colonists. Instead they found a delightful haven. The supposedly uninhabitable island of devils abounded in fowl, eggs, hogs, and fruit; it had no snakes or rodents; and it offered an excellent harbor and an ideal climate. For more than nine months the passengers and crew of *Sea Venture* lived primitively but comfortably. One marriage took place, and two children were born, a boy, Bermudas Eason, and a girl, Bermuda Rolfe. Only five persons died. Eventually all but three men, left behind to secure England's claim to the island, sailed for Virginia in two pinnaces built under the supervision of Admiral Somers from salvaged cedar planks and ship's gear. The survivors arrived at Jamestown on 24 May 1610, almost a year after their departure from England.

During that year the Virginia colony had suffered cruelly. The great Gates expedition, minus the flagship and the foundered vessel, straggled into Chesapeake Bay more in need of relief than able to give it. Most of the ships and their cargoes had severe sea damage, and because of the earlier exaggerated reports of Virginia's plentitude, the four hundred passengers came ill-prepared for the rigors of the wilderness. Drastic shortages of food and shelter would soon devastate the colony, but for the moment the chief shortage seemed to lie in leadership and good will. The newcomers knew that the government would be reconstituted on Gates' arrival, which — because the fate of *Sea Venture* was unknown — they expected shortly, and so they paid little attention to President Smith. He, in turn, had nothing but contempt for the aristocrats "of good meanes, and great parentage" who snubbed the rough soldier, perhaps because he "gave not any due respect to many worthy Gentlemen." Factions rapidly emerged. Most of the seamen favored Smith, a man no doubt more to their liking than the gentlemen they had recently seen too much of at sea. Another group clustered around George Percy, the "old planter" of highest social rank, though, according to one report, "none . . . would pay him much heed." In sum, "every man overvaluing his own worth, would be a Commander: every man underprising an others value, denied to be commanded."

President Smith still held nominal authority, and he did his best to procure supplies from the Indians and to distribute the settlers in groups large enough to defend themselves yet small enough to gather food efficiently. He sent Percy, Martin, and sixty men to the Nansemond River, near the mouth of the James. He also dispatched Captain Francis West, twenty-two year old brother of Lord de la Warr, with 140 men to the James River falls. But if dispersal of the settlers alleviated some of the colony's problems, it exacerbated others, especially Indian-white relations.

The tribes near Jamestown had become so friendly before the arrival of the third supply that they were ready to fight beside the English against a feared Spanish attack. A few weeks later the natives, with good reason, had again taken the warpath against the colony. At Nansemond, a misunderstanding arose between the colonists and the local tribe, whereupon Captain Martin seized the chief's house and corn. The resulting retaliation took several English lives. At the falls, some of the irresponsible settlers despoiled the Indians, "stealing their corne, robbing their gardens, beating them, breaking their houses and keeping some prisoners." The Indians complained to Smith that rather than protecting them, as by treaty the English were bound to do, the settlers at the falls had become the Indians' worst enemies. The local chiefs "desired pardon if hereafter they defended themselves" and begged Smith to lead them against their tormentors. Smith spent several days at the falls trying to reform West's men, but as soon as he left the Indians attacked the fort and killed several Englishmen.

At this point Smith's enemies felt strong enough to oust him from office. "Perhaps you shall have it blazoned a mutenie" Gabriel Archer wrote to a friend in England, and in a sense it was. Smith legally held command, for the new charter and instructions had not yet arrived. But a coalition of Archer, Ratcliffe, West, and Martin summarily ended the relatively successful but autocratic rule of John Smith. And since he could not be voted out by the existing council — all its members having died — he could only be deposed by a frontier coup d'etat.

Exactly how it happened is blurred by conflicting accounts. Smith's enemies placed the blame on him, although they disagreed about the circumstances. One accused him of plotting to have Powhatan kill Captain West; another insisted that Smith had been "sent home to answere some misdeamenors"; while George Percy, who succeeded Smith, charged him with being "an Ambityous, unworthy and vayneglorious fellowe" who was deposed for ruling without a council. Smith's version — published in his *Generall Historie,* though he attributed the authorship of that section to others — tells another side of the story. Smith, it contends, held the reins until his year in office had about expired and then elected Martin to the post, who "knowing his owne insufficiency, and the companies untowardnesse and little regard of him," resigned in three hours. Smith resumed the helm for several weeks more, when an accidental explosion of his powder bag wounded him severely. Taking advantage of his feeble condition, an anti-Smith cabal tried to murder the captain as he lay semiconscious in his bed. The intended assassination weapon misfired. Its message, however, got through to Smith; half-alive and surrounded by enemies he no longer had strength to combat, he took ship for England. One point is clear from every account: the colony's leaders, for whatever reason, had had enough of John Smith. In early October 1609 he left Virginia, never to return.

With Smith gone matters rapidly deteriorated. Powhatan's fear of and respect for the captain, already eroded by the events of the previous months, no longer shielded the colony. Seventeen of Martin's men at Nansemond went to Kecoughtan to barter for food and were never heard of again; a few days later the bodies of several other Englishmen were found, "their mowthes stopped full of Breade" as a warning to the colonists to seek sustenance at peril of their lives. Soon after, Captain West withdrew his plantation to Jamestown; he had lost eleven more men to the Indians. With supplies low, Percy in desperation sent Captain Ratcliffe to Powhatan to barter for corn and other commodities. At first negotiations looked promising, but in the end Ratcliffe's credulity and Powhatan's animosity combined to bring further disaster to the faltering colony. Ratcliffe might have ensured his own safety by detaining on his boat a son and daughter of the chief, but he trustingly let them go. He also allowed small groups of his men to enter the Indian houses, whereupon "the Slye owlde kinge" ordered a massacre of the Englishmen. Ratcliffe was taken alive, bound naked to a tree, and, according to George Percy's report, "by woemen his fleshe was skraped from his bones with mussell shelles and befre his face throwne into the fyer. And so for want of circumspection [he] miserably perished." Of the fifty men who had left Jamestown under Ratcliffe, only sixteen returned.

Close to starvation, the colonists became increasingly desperate. Captain West with thirty-six men in *Swallow* managed to get a boatload of corn at Potomac, but only through "some harshe and Crewell dealinge," and by decapitating two Indians — which, as an anonymous pamphleteer admitted, "created the *Indians* our implacable enemies. . . ." But rather than relieving the men at Jamestown, West hoisted sail for England, leaving the stunned settlers in an even worse plight. "A worlde of miseries ensewed," Percy sadly reported. The starving colonists ate every living animal, even dogs, cats, mice, and serpents; then clothing and shoe leather. Some wandered into the woods for roots, only to be slain by the Indians; others sought haven with the natives and were never heard of again. A few hunger-crazed men broke into the storehouse, where Percy had laid aside a small reserve against the coming winter; he had them executed. There were other, more gruesome, victims of judicial vengeance. One man murdered his pregnant wife, cut her in pieces, "and salted her for his foode." Percy hanged the culprit by his thumbs with weights at his feet until he confessed, then burned him to death. Percy executed another for feeding on human corpses, for the colonists "weare driven through unsufferable hunger unnaturallie to eat those things which nature most abhorred, the flesh and excrements of man, as well of owne nation as of an Indian, digged by some out of his grave after [he] had laien buried three daies & wholly devoured him." Before the frightful winter ended, starvation, disease, and Indian arrows had taken an appalling toll. There were five hundred colonists in Virginia when John Smith departed for England in October 1609; only sixty remained six months later.

By that time the loss of Smith to the colony had become bitterly poignant. He had at least preserved life and a semblance of cooperation. Percy, himself "so sicke hee could neither goe nor stand," lacked imagination as well as forcefulness. Perhaps Smith could not have palliated the natives, and undoubtedly he could not have turned scarcity into abundance, but he would not have permitted, as did Percy, near starvation at Jamestown while only thirty miles away at Point Comfort a small group under Captain Davis lived comfortably on crabs and hogs. Not until May 1610 did Percy realize that by shifting the whole colony to Point Comfort he could relieve much of the suffering. He was on the verge of moving his people when two small ships came into sight. On board were Sir Thomas Gates, Sir George Somers, Captain Christopher Newport, and the other survivors of *Sea Venture*. Each party must have been cruelly surprised at the other's condition. Instead of the thriving colony of several hundred that the Bermuda refugees expected, they found barely sixty pathetic beings who "Looked Lyke Anotamies Cryeinge owtt we are starved We are starved." The colony, desperately in need of succor itself, now had 150 more mouths to feed. Assuming Virginia to be flourishing, Gates had brought from Bermuda only enough provisions for his voyage.

All the shortcomings of English efforts in Virginia — the failures of leadership in the colony, of planning by the company, of dealings with the Indians, of selection of a place for settlement — had combined to bring this attempt at New World colonization to ruin. Governor Gates could not begin to follow his elaborate instructions; the only practical option he had was to abandon the colony. A hasty check on provisions showed barely enough for sixteen days — too little to reach England and too little to hold out until summer crops could be harvested. After making all remaining flour into sea biscuit and loading all salvageable goods, Gates reluctantly but wisely ordered all hands aboard the four small ships that alone offered escape. Two hundred-odd men, women, and children embarked at Jamestown on 7 June 1610, barely three years since the arrival of the initial expedition to Virginia. (Governor Gates boarded last to prevent the bitter remnant from burning the village, an act of destruction that might deny useful shelter to future expeditions.) With luck Jamestown's survivors could reach Newfoundland before their rations expired; there the half-starved settlers would find fishing ships to feed them and carry them home to England. The attempt to plant the "Firste Colonie" seemingly had failed.

At the very moment Gates and his followers evacuated Jamestown, Thomas West, Baron de la Warr, arrived at Point Comfort where a small garrison waited to be picked up by Gates on his way out of the bay. On learning of the plan to evacuate Virginia, de la Warr sent his long boat up river to intercept Gates. Virginia was saved, for de la Warr had not come empty-handed. His fleet carried three hundred healthy passengers and a year's supply of provisions. It also carried, in the person of de la Warr, a man selected by the London Company to give Britain's American outpost new life and direction.

Governor de la Warr at once took firm hold. He knew, as Smith did, that regardless of Virginia's natural abundance men must be constructively busy in order to keep not only the benefits of their labor but, in times of despair, the will to live. During the starving time, George Percy reported, some men "goeinge to bedd as we imagined in healthe weare fownd deade the nexte morneinge." He also noted that in the midst of crisis, Captain Daniel Tucker built with his own hands a sizable boat, which gave "A little Reliefe unto us And did kepe us from killinge one of An other." Smith had allowed no loafers to undermine the colony's morale or their own mental health, nor did de la Warr. He immediately assembled the colonists in the half-razed Jamestown church and announced strict rules. Blaming much of Jamestown's troubles on the "Idlenes of our owne people," the new governor threatened to punish severely any future indolence. He also divided the company into groups of fifty, with a captain in charge of each. Every man was assigned a task at which he must "worke painefully," although that description should not be taken too literally; the governor's schedule, like Smith's, required only six hours of labor per day, 6 to 10 A.M. and 2 to 4 P.M. But even the gentlemen had to work, though at planning and supervising rather than laboring. New houses went up, fields were cleared, and the French vintners — brought by de la Warr — planted vines. Other men worked on two new forts, Henry and Charles (named "in honor of our most noble Prince and his hopefull brother") on a hill near Southampton River (now Hampton River). There, where the air, water, and fields seemed more wholesome than at Jamestown, all new-comers would be housed on arrival, "that the wearisomnes of the sea may bee refreshed in this pleasing part of the coun-trey." Meanwhile Sir George Somers and Captain Argall sailed to Bermuda for a cargo of hogs to replenish the Virginia stock. And although Somers died on the island and his crew went on to England, Argall sailed north "where he hapned upon some fishe" which he brought back to Jamestown. Dissension, once so virile, gradually subsided.

Only Indian relations remained unchanged by the new regime. The tide of battle, however, swung in favor of the English. Gates led an expedition against the village of Kecoughtan, lured the natives into the open with a drum and dance act by one of his soldiers, and slaughtered them. Simi-larly, when Powhatan refused to relinquish men and arma-ments captured during the starving time, returning instead "prowde and disdaynefull Answers," Percy took seventy men and an Indian guide ("whome the provoste marshall ledd in A hande locke") in a surprise attack on the village of the Paspa-heghs. The troops killed fifteen or sixteen Indians and cap-tured several, including the local queen, her children, and a brave. Percy admonished his lieutenant for taking any prison-ers at all, especially an adult male; less squeamish than his sub-ordinate, the commander "cawsed the Indians heade to be cut of." After destroying the village and fields, Percy's soldiers "did begin to murmur becawse the quene and her Children were spared. . . . A Cowncell beinge called itt was Agreed upon to putt the Children to deathe the which was effected by Thoweinge them overboard and shoteinge owtt their Braynes in the water." Percy managed with difficulty to keep his men from killing the queen too, but she only survived long enough for Lord de la Warr to order her burned at the stake. Percy convinced the governor to let her be more mercifully executed. She died by the sword.

Ambushes and atrocities continued on both sides. Contingents of English soldiers laid waste to Indian villages. A party of Englishmen searching for iron mines succumbed to offers of food and fell victim to Indians who well remembered Gates' use of a drummer as decoy. Several years would pass before a reconciliation between the races occurred.

Otherwise, Virginia once again took on the appearance of a viable extension of the British Isles. By mid-summer of 1610 the resident council wrote to the London Company that most matters looked highly promising. Despite ill-trained men, the prospects for wine-making appeared bright, and more land for farming and hunting would soon be available — to be taken from the Indians in revenge for their hostility. The company also had hopeful testimony from deputy-governor Sir Thomas Gates, called back to England for consultation and advice. Whether Gates had a spell of excessive optimism brought on by deliverance from his long series of misfortunes, or whether the company unreasonably inflated Gates' reports when issuing its *True Declaration of the estate of the Colonie in Virginia* (1610) cannot now be known, but its author certainly indulged his imagination by placing the future of the American outpost on a plane with Caesar's France and Alexander's Greece.

Such predictions were decidedly premature. Lord de la Warr could control his colonists, and he could curb the Indians, but he had no power over the diseases that wracked his body. "A hote and violent Ague" struck him shortly after his arrival at Jamestown, and he never fully recovered. Dr. Lawrence Bohune, resident physician, relieved some of his lordship's blood. The governor thought that helped a good deal, but he soon suffered a relapse accompanied by flux,

cramps, gout, and scurvy. For much of his stay in Virginia
Lord de la Warr lived aboard ship where his subordinates had
to seek him for decisions and directives. Fearing for his life if
he remained longer in Virginia, in late March of 1611 de la
Warr headed for Nevis in the West Indies, "famous for wholesome Bathes." When winds blew his ship off course he decided
to go on to England where full recovery seemed most possible.
He left George Percy behind as lieutenant governor.

De la Warr's unexpected return embarrassed the company,
then in the midst of a frantic propaganda campaign to restore
the Virginia venture to public esteem. Characteristically, the
company tried to turn a handicap into an asset by printing de
la Warr's defense of his conduct. The governor justified deser-
tion of his post on the grounds of personal survival, then used
the rest of his tract to praise Virginia's prospects and to
encourage investors who had lately shown "coldnesse and
irresolution" toward the project. The colony had never looked
more promising, he insisted, with more than two hundred
settlers living there comfortably, and with agriculture, fishing,
and trade with the Indians all improving rapidly.

If it did not change the company's sagging reputation overnight, the governor's encouraging report at least reinforced its
efforts at public relations. Since the disasters of 1609–1610 the
company had aimed a barrage of pamphlets and broadsides at
potential investors and colonists. There was no escaping the
fact of the shipwreck on Bermuda nor the agony of the starving time. But the implications of those events could, if reported skillfully, be minimized and even turned to advantage.
The wreck of *Sea Venture,* for example, could be presented as
a sign of God's favor to British colonization. Had not all
hands survived? And had not England discovered a beautiful
island for additional colonization? The starving time did not
lend itself to such rationalization, but a clever pamphleteer
could divert blame from the company and insist that such a
unique calamity could not happen again. The *True Declaration* of 1610 deplored the false rumors and biased reports that

had misrepresented affairs in Virginia. The temporary loss of Thomas Gates had, it admitted, "separated the head from the bodie"; the colonists' health had been undermined by "the brackish water of *James* fort"; and covetous mariners had damaged the colony by embezzling provisions and glutting the Indian trade. But the basic problem had been the settlers themselves. They had been too shortsighted to salt fish and repair their nets, too indolent to tend to their crops and buildings, and too heedless of God's wrath. Sin and idleness, idleness and sin. The solution was self-evident: henceforth the company would send "none but honest sufficient Aritificers, as Carpenters, Smiths, Coopers, Fishermen, Brickmen, and such like." John Smith undoubtedly read with a mixture of approval and bitterness the repeated insistence that no "idle and wicked persons" would be accepted anymore; the company now required each candidate for emigration to apply in person and present "some good testimony of his religion to God, and civil manners and behaviour to his neighbour. . . ." Similarly, the broadside advertising an expedition in the spring of 1611 rebuffed "vagrant and unnecessarie persons"; none but the "honest and industrious" need apply.

To make sure that its latest recruits conformed to its expectations, the company revamped the colony's laws and appointed a new official to enforce them. On 12 May 1611, a ship carrying Sir Thomas Dale, marshall and deputy governor, dropped anchor off Point Comfort. Dale's arrival would not bring good cheer or prosperity to Virginia. It would, however, bring an unprecedented degree of orderliness and industry, qualities that the colony had largely ignored except for the brief administrations of John Smith and Lord de la Warr. But a new regime would not find the task any easier than had Smith. During his two years in Virginia Captain Smith had been able to coerce his men partly because the colony was small enough for him to keep an eye on everyone, and partly because every man could see that Smith drove himself as hard as he drove others. As the colony grew, new problems of administration, both political and economic, once again threatened to undermine the best of intentions. Although shunned by the company, Captain Smith, through his writings, kept England informed of the continuing plight of its American settlement.

MATOAKA ALS REBECCA FILIA POTENTISS PRINC POWHATANI IMP VIRGINIÆ

Pocahontas, sometimes called Matoaka,
after her conversion and marriage

V

Search for Stability: Politics and Diplomacy

DURING its first four years the Virginia venture had failed to meet three basic needs: political stability, economic prosperity, and peaceful Indian relations. All were essential to the colony's survival, yet only under John Smith had they been simultaneously met, and then briefly and very imperfectly. Smith had brought some political order, made some progress toward a viable economy, and kept a tenuous peace with the Indians, albeit a peace based on the natives' awe of him. But his policies depended too greatly on one man's will. With Smith gone, the colony's stability collapsed. The wreck of the *Sea Venture* and de la Warr's illness thwarted the company's efforts during the next two years. Virginia now needed, the London Company concluded, a firm set of laws, stringent economic regulations, and controls that would encourage the Indians to remain peaceful and cooperative no matter who held the governorship. Between 1611 and 1618 the colony moved toward these objectives, though not always in ways the company expected or desired.

To implement its latest policies the company once again sent new men to administer the colony, additional settlers to swell the shrunken population, and fresh supplies to replace the losses of the previous years. The first installment of human and material cargo arrived with Sir Thomas Dale, whose fleet brought three hundred passengers, cattle, and a year's provisions in May 1611. A few months later Sir Thomas Gates arrived, for a second time, with three hundred more settlers, one hundred cows, and additional provisions. By the fall of 1611 the colony's material support from England seemed adequate if not sumptuous. Still, shortages and shortcomings continued, frustrating planters and adventurers alike.

Dale, who replaced Percy as acting governor, had expected to find Lord de la Warr in charge, adequate food in the colony, and busy and productive residents. But de la Warr had left ten days earlier; the spring planting had not been calculated to feed so many new settlers; and the residents had become a colony of "disordered persons, so prophane, so riotous, so full of Mutenie and treasonable Intendments." They were blithely engaged in "their daily and usuall workes, bowling in the streetes," their dilapidated houses "ready to fall upon their heads." And Dale's own cargo of men proved little better. Because of excessive crowding in the voyage over, death and disease had been high, even though he had made the journey in less than eight weeks. Then the oppressive summer climate took its toll of health and energy. And despite the company's attempt to screen applicants, the character of the latest contingent to Virginia fell far short of expectations. Soon after his arrival Dale complained to Lord Salisbury that only sixty of the three hundred who came with him could or would work.

Making maximum use of the able workers, Dale did his best to remedy a potentially critical situation. He assigned some men to plant a late crop of corn at Point Comfort; others to repair the church and the storehouse at Jamestown, to construct stables, a powderhouse, a wharf for unloading ships, and to dig a new well; and still others to strengthen the forts, sow flax and hemp, and build a blockhouse to protect English cattle. The list of things to be done seemed endless. Not least was the construction of a new town near the head of the falls. Named after Henry, Prince of Wales, Henrico served briefly as the largest and most solidly constructed town in Virginia. Within a few months of his arrival Dale had the colony in its best physical condition since John Smith's departure. But Dale's problems had only begun. While he had shown commendable skill in restoring the material condition of the colony, he proved less adept in coping with its human welfare.

Sir Thomas Dale's most questionable policy was to implement rigorously a new code of justice, the *Lawes Divine, Morall and Martiall*. He had little to do with the drafting and promulgation of the most notorious parts of the code, but as marshall of the colony he enforced the new rules with appalling harshness. In his determination to bring order to the colony, Dale showed excessive zeal that in the long run did more harm than good to England's colonial enterprise.

The *Lawes Divine, Morall and Martiall* came initially from the London Company. The Crown's instructions in 1606 had insisted that the law in Virginia follow "as neer to the common lawes of England and the equity thereof as may be." But a series of inexperienced presidents and councils had administered law and justice as each had seen fit, with consequent vacillation, uncertainty, and inequity. By 1609 the company realized the need for strict discipline in Virginia because the uncooperative settlers would not willingly channel their energy into useful pursuits. The leaders in the colony concurred. In 1610 Governor de la Warr and his council lamented that so many of the colonists had "distempered bodies and infected mindes, whome no examples . . . either of goodnes or punishment, can deterr from their habituall impieties. . . ." Accordingly, Gates, and then de la Warr, imposed regulations drafted largely by Gates in the aftermath of the starving time, though very likely along lines prescribed by the company before they set sail. Shortly after Dale arrived, he issued an enlarged version of those laws. They were subsequently recorded by William Strachey, secretary of the colony in 1610–1611, who carried copies home to

England in September of the latter year. With the blessing of the London Company, which at the time needed to show prospective investors that it had taken firm action to bring order to the notoriously unruly colonists, Strachey in 1612 published a codified version of the laws.

Most of the *Lawes Divine, Morall and Martiall* dealt with military matters and were almost certainly the work of Dale, fashioned in accordance with prevailing custom. Their basic contents and format came from the military codes used for decades by English commanders in the Low Countries. Dale, as well as Gates and de la Warr, had served in the Netherlands and had intimate knowledge of the military regulations imposed on overseas Englishmen. Dale tailored such codes to the American scene: "No Souldier may speake or have any private conference with any of the salvages without leave of his Captaine, nor his Captaine without leave of his chiefe Officer, upon paine of death," read section 38; while number 45 threatened death to anyone who without authorization maltreated an Indian or his property. The long list of capital crimes was not unduly severe for military regulations of its day nor, in fact, for centuries thereafter.

The civil and criminal provisions of "Dale's Code" also followed prevailing patterns: the death penalty for outspoken impiety, traitorous speech, theft, a third conviction for blasphemy, and for illegal trade with Indians or with English seamen. The code prescribed whippings or imprisonment for other serious offenses. The punishments for many lesser crimes were more unique and more brutal: a bodkin thrust through the tongue for a second offense of blasphemy, six months as a galley-slave for a third unexcused absence from daily divine service, and a month with head and feet tied together every night for uttering "any disgracefull words" against the colony or its residents. The code authorized ear-cropping for the first offense by bakers who "use any dishonest and deceiptfull tricke to make the bread weigh heavier"; cooks and fishermen suffered similar punishments for not rendering true accounts.

Because the penalties for disobeying the *Lawes Divine, Morall and Martiall* had sufficient precedents, the hue and cry that eventually surrounded them came not so much from the written code as from its application. Dale had imbibed little of the milk of human kindness. When several men ran away to the Indians, he had them retaken and executed, and he showed as little mercy for men or women convicted of other crimes. He arrested two women, assigned to sew shirts for the colony's servants, for making some of theirs too short, "for which fact the said *Anne leyden* and *Jane wright* were whipt, And *Anne leyden* beinge then with childe (the same night thereof miscarried) ."

Even hardened settlers deplored such severity. George Percy had often seen cruelty in Virginia but was shocked by Dale's handling of the colony's criminals: "Some he apointed to be hanged Some burned Some to be broken upon wheles, others to be staked and some to be shott to deathe . . . and some which Robbed the store he cawsed them to be bownd faste unto Trees and so sterved them to deathe." Twelve years later the Virginia House of Burgesses corroborated Percy's account and charged that men had fled to the Indians only because Dale allowed them insufferable rations, "mouldy, rotten, full of Cobwebs and Maggotts loathsome to man and not fytt for beasts." According to the Assembly's "Tragicall Relation," under Dale the sick suffered as unduly as the criminal, through excessive application of the no work–no food principle. The assembly reported that "Many through these extremities, being weery of life, digged holes in the earth and there hidd themselves till they famished." Most serious of all, perhaps, for Virginia's prospects as an integral part of the British empire and thus as a home for permanent settlement, was the charge that the executions were "often times without tryall or Judgment." Dale had dispensed with trial by jury as well as customary English laws and penalties.

Even Dale's supporters acknowledged the fundamental accusations against him. Ralph Hamor, for example, denied that

Dale had been tyrannous or even severe, contending that the criminals had been "dangerous, incurable members, for no use so fit as to make examples to others," and defended Dale by insisting that France and other countries indulged in equally barbarous practices. Hamor admitted, however, that Dale imposed penalties more severe than were usual in England. Therein lay the principal charge against Thomas Dale and the company. Englishmen had been promised English rights; instead Dale subjected them to martial law, wielded with a vengeance. Prospective colonists could take small comfort from the company's claim that harsh punishments had been used exclusively to frighten potential offenders for whom "the feare of a cruell, painefull and unusuall death, more refrains them then death it selfe."

The ruthless policies of Dale and of Gates, who in August 1611 relieved him as acting governor but not as marshall, rested on the assumption that the colony's plight necessitated stringent discipline. At home, society had a steadying influence. Family, church, community, and government guided personal and group behavior. Virginia had few such controls: almost no families, few clergymen, scattered and unstable communities, and an unpredictable government that took its orders from a commercial organization three thousand miles away. Throughout its first decade, Virginia was essentially a military post serving a trading company. All of the colony's leaders and many of its followers were professional soldiers, recruited to defend the American foothold and to impose order on its inhabitants.

Convinced that the colony had become a place for "Parents to disburden themselves of lascivious sonnes, masters of bad servants and wives of ill husbands," the company had resorted to martial law "as of most dispatch and terror and fittest for this government." The settlers remained recalcitrant. Reverend Patrick Copland, a stockholder and leading spokesman, later reported that "they neglected God's worship, lived in idlenesse, plodded conspiracies, resisted the governement of

Superiors, and carried themselves dissolutely amongst the heathens." To make the colonists work and to make them observe England's religious and civil mores — lest they succumb to anarchy as in the starving time or to "savagery" by joining the Indians — required stern measures. Even the worst of men, the company believed, could be made into good citizens through "severe discipline . . . sharpe lawes, a hard life and much labour." Hence the *Lawes Divine, Morall and Martiall*. Hence too the collective paranoia that gripped Virginia's leaders as they struggled to preserve England's only American colony.

Virginians in the early years feared most, yet confronted least, an attack by Spain. The threat did not lack substance. Through its representatives in London and spies along the Atlantic coast, the Spanish court closely watched the growth of British America. Had conditions been slightly different on several occasions, his Most Catholic Majesty would have crushed in the bud the young Virginia plant. But Virginia was saved by its very ineptitude. A colony that consisted of a few squalid houses, killed off its inhabitants as fast as they arrived, produced nothing but controversy, and could not plausibly assault his American territories, presented no threat to the King of Spain. He simply could not bother to destroy it.

The Virginians did not know that. Repeatedly during the early decades the colonists seized arms to repel a fancied invasion by Spanish ships, only to discover that the approaching sails hung from English spars. In 1609, for example, John Smith took alarm at a fleet that turned out to be the Gates-Somers expedition (minus *Sea Venture*) arriving from England with the third supply. Similarly, in 1611 Thomas Dale prepared to resist a squadron that in fact carried his superior, Sir Thomas Gates, instead of Spanish soldiers. The company in London felt almost as nervous as the colonists in Virginia. It could do little to resist an attack, but at least the company could, and did, try to allay any impression that the colony had

aggressive designs on Spanish territory. When in 1618 the Earl
of Warwick sent a ship into the West Indies to prey on
Spanish vessels, the company quickly disavowed any connec-
tion with the episode lest it bring retaliation against the
colony.

Throughout the first quarter-century of British colonization, Spain toyed with the idea of an expedition against
Jamestown. Don Pedro de Zuñiga, ambassador to the Court of
St. James from 1605 to 1610, and his successor, Don Alonso de
Valasco, frequently advised Madrid that the fledgling colony
must be uprooted before it grew too strong. "It would be a
service to God for Your majesty to stop a villainy and a
swindle like this," Zuñiga urged. He and other Spaniards
suspected that England intended more than a colony for
dumping surplus population; long-range English policy, they
believed, aimed at eventual control of most of the Atlantic
coast and of the Pacific or South Sea in order to intercept
Spanish treasure ships. Rumors in 1609 that Sir Walter Ralegh
would soon be released from the Tower of London to lead an
expedition to Guiana added to Spanish apprehensions.
Prodded by fears of English encirclement, Spain's Council for
the Indies recommended in 1612 that a small force attack the
English at Jamestown "before they take more root and possess
themselves of more land. . . ." But Philip III's Council of
State concluded that Virginia presented no menace and
should therefore be left alone. It had no gold, no silver, and in
its pathetic condition could hardly be a base for raids on
Spanish territory.

So accurate an assessment of Virginia resulted from close
Spanish surveillance of the colony. Some information came
from England where Spanish officials had long been adept at
gathering intelligence, though not always accurately. More
reliable word came from the colony itself. Spain may have had
an informer in the first resident council; Captain George
Kendall's execution in the fall of 1607 resulted partly from
allegations that he, as an English Catholic, intended to help

Spain destroy the colony. At about the same time, the Spanish colony in Florida sent Indian spies to Jamestown and a reconnaissance party under Captain Francisco Fernandez de Ecija. Spain also tried more direct infiltration. In 1611 an expedition under Captain Diego de Molina sailed from Lisbon to reconnoiter the Jamestown area. Near Point Comfort the captain and two companions walked into an English ambush and were captured, although the remaining Spaniards also seized a prisoner in the scuffle. From the English prisoner the Spanish forced a fairly accurate description of the colony. The English learned from the captive Spaniard what they already suspected: Spain had an eye on Virginia and might assault it at any time.

Concerned by the colony's improved health, the Council for the Indies in 1611 favored an attack as soon as possible, waiting only for further intelligence from America. This, the council believed, could best be gotten by sending two English Jesuits, then at seminaries in Spain, to England, where in the guise of colonists they would sail to Virginia. As soon as the priests could collect their information and return to Spain, an expedition would be mounted against the colony. Fortunately for the future of British America the plan never came to fruition, because Philip continued to believe that the English were throwing good money after bad.

The threat to early Virginia helps to explain why Dale and Gates tried hard to settle, however hastily, their disputes with Chief Powhatan. An Indian assault from the interior while the Spanish attacked from the sea would surely doom the colony. To lessen that possibility, Dale determined to bring Powhatan to his knees. Writing to Lord Salisbury in August 1611, Dale vowed that he would "so over master the subtile-mischeivous Great Powhatan, that I should leave him either no room in his Countrie to harbour in, or drawe him to a firme association with ourselves. . . ." Dale proposed to clear the Indians from the triangle of land bordered by the James and York rivers and the fall line, an area about twelve miles by one-hundred fifty, and containing "the principallest Seates of Powhatan."

The plan was not easily accomplished. Powhatan's men continually harassed Englishmen trying to make new settlements in the interior, and once so confounded Dale's garrison at the falls that the colonists began to assault each other. That episode, along with some other Indian tricks, convinced Reverend Alexander Whitaker that "there be great witches amongest them and they [are] very familiar with the divill." It took more than a little witchcraft to deter Dale. As soon as he had the internal affairs of the colony "well settled and ordered," he led one hundred men against the Nansemond tribe. Both sides suffered casualties, and Dale himself came close to being killed by an arrow that glanced off his helmet. ("If itt had fallen A thowght Lower," Percy quipped, it "mightt have Shott him into the Braynes and indangered his Lyfe.") The victory soon went to the English, who for the first time in Virginia used large numbers of men in full armor. Seeing that their weapons could not damage the English, the Indians "did fall into their exorcismes conjuracyons and charmes[,] throweinge fyer upp into the skyes[,] Runneinge up and downe with Rattles and makeinge many dyabolicall gestures with many irigramantcke Spelles and incantacionus. . . ." Heedless of both arrows and incantations, Dale destroyed the natives' houses and crops and seized several captives. Still the Indians assaulted stragglers near Henrico, and parties of Englishmen could not venture from the fort without armed guards.

Two years passed before Gates and Dale found a way to stabilize Indian-English relations. The solution, or at least the first stage of it, looked like a page out of John Smith's book — a combination of bullying Chief Powhatan and exploiting (in Dale's case at least) Princess Pocahontas. Pocahontas had remained friendly to the English, although with Smith gone and racial hostility rampant, the "nonpareil" of Virginia no longer visited the settlements. Then Captain Samuel Argall, back in the colony after a trip to old England and an expedition against the French in New England, offered a bold and cynical plan by which Pocahontas could again be used to English advantage.

Powhatan still held eight English prisoners and numerous English tools and weapons. Threats did him no harm, and in the face of an offensive attack he only moved temporarily inland. Argall therefore proposed to seize *"Powhatans* delight and darling, his daughter *Pocahuntas"* and hold her until the chief met the colony's terms. Argall confessed to a friend his resolve "to possesse myselfe of her by any strategm that I could use."

One of the least admirable characters in early Virginia history, Argall was not above using threats, bribery, and kidnapping. He soon found his chance by exploiting Indian rivalries. The Princess lived at that time in the household of the King of Potomac, a chief not under Powhatan's control and on good terms with the colony. Threatened with the loss of English friendship, the Potomac chief agreed to betray Pocahontas. With the help of two other Indians who joined the plot for "a small Copper kettle, and som other les valuable toies," Argall lured Pocahontas on board his ship. He then sent a messenger to tell Powhatan that the English held her hostage.

After three months of silence Powhatan acquiesced. He sent several English captives, some weapons and tools, and a canoe-load of corn to Jamestown. Gates and his advisors were not satisfied. They suspected Powhatan of withholding other English property and of enticing some newly released captives back to his village — who may, of course, have preferred the freedom of Indian society to the rigorous discipline of Dale's Jamestown. In March 1613 Dale and Argall led a shipload of soldiers up Powhatan's river, with the captive Pocahontas on board. Dale put the challenge bluntly: Powhatan could either fight for his daughter or restore the remaining English goods and give the colony five hundred bushels of corn. For a while it appeared that the Indians preferred to fight. Several skirmishes took place, but because their arms were no match for European weapons, Powhatan avoided an open clash. Eventually the English withdrew, leaving another ultimatum: meet Dale's demands by harvest time or his troops would return to destroy and kill at random. Pocahontas remained in custody.

"Long before this time," Ralph Hamor wrote in 1614, "a gentleman of approved behaviour and honest cariage, maister John *Rolfe* had bin in love with *Pocahuntas* and she with him. . . ." Rolfe's first wife had died sometime after their arrival in Virginia. He apparently found solace in instructing Pocahontas in Christianity during her captivity; and her command of English and Dale's determination to make a convert, regardless of the lives he took in the process, made her a ready subject for proselytizing. In any event, a deep affection developed between the "honest and discreete English Gentleman" and the Indian princess. Rolfe determined to marry her.

The first and most famous union of the English and Indians took place only after Rolfe secured the approval of the highest authority in the colony. In early 1614, while negotiations with Powhatan dragged on, Rolfe addressed a formal request to deputy-governor Dale (who had reassumed leadership of the colony when Gates again sailed for England) asking permission to marry Pocahontas. Rolfe's statement reveals much about the social protocol of early Virginia as well as the inner feelings of a passionate man in an almost womanless society. Rolfe insisted that he wanted to marry Pocahontas for the salvation of her soul and benefit of the plantation; he offered himself as a model of "innocency and godly ferver," entirely free of the venal motives attributed to him by "the vulgar sort." But he protested too much. His letter shows the torment of a lusty, lonely middle-aged Englishman who had fallen in love with a maiden whom he desperately desired but who failed to meet the standards of his society. Only the most selfless motives — the glory of God, the honor of England and its plantation, and "the converting of one unregenerate, to regeneration" — Rolfe insisted, would permit him "to be in love with one whose education hath bin rude, her manners barbarous, her generation accursed, and so discrepant in all nurtriture from my selfe. . . ." His letter to Dale poignantly revealed why so few marriages took place between whites and Indians: the cultural and religious gap loomed too large in the English mind. Because of Pocahontas' long attachment to the English, and because she had, according to Dale, "renounced publickly her countrey Idolatry" and been baptized a Christian, she became an exception. There would be few others in the long history of British America.

To the delight of the Virginia colonists, the affection between Rolfe and Pocahontas had an immediate and benign influence on racial relations. Secretary Ralph Hamor reported that the impending marriage caused Governor Dale to soften his demands on Powhatan, while Pocahontas urged her father and brothers to meet the English terms. After some hesitation, Powhatan submitted. Sometime in April 1614, at the Jamestown church, Reverend Richard Bucke joined Pocahontas and John Rolfe in marriage. Powhatan refused to attend but gave his blessing to the union and sent an uncle of Pocahontas to give the bride away.

During the brief remainder of Pocahontas' life and for several years thereafter, Powhatan and his successors, Itopatan and Opechancanough, dealt peacefully with their white neighbors. And there is no doubt that the marriage of Powhatan's daughter played an important role in the mutual good will of those years. About a month after the wedding, Dale dispatched Ralph Hamor to visit the aging chief, who eagerly inquired about the bridal couple, "how they liked, lived and loved together." Dale sent along a variety of gifts and promised more; in return he hoped the chief could send another of his daughters to be the governor's "neerest companion, wife and bedfellow." This, Dale predicted, would further cement the friendship of Englishmen and Indians and prove that the two peoples could now be one. Unfortunately for such a worthy cause, Powhatan's other daughter had previously been pledged to a native chief. Besides, Powhatan pointed out, the English already had one of his daughters, and "I holde it not a brotherly part of your King, to desire to bereave me of two of my children at once."

In his confrontations with the English Powhatan was more worn out than won over. He had fought them until his losses mounted to an alarming total; then they seized Pocahontas as hostage. She had, of her own volition, renounced her heritage, married an Englishman, and become a member of the enemy society. In deference to his daughter, he would fight no longer. The chief had resolved, Hamor reported, "upon no terms whatsoever to put himselfe into our hands, or come amongst us. . . ." Yet Powhatan promised never again to make war against the English, even on just provocation, "for I am now olde," he told Hamor, "and would gladly end my daies in peace, so as if the English offer me injury, my country is large enough. I will remove my selfe farther from you." The Virginia colonists had at last gotten the peace they wanted, and on their own terms. But Powhatan's pledge would die with him, only a few years later, and the passing of both Pocahontas and her father would set the stage for renewed hostilities.

In the meantime, Virginia enjoyed its most prolonged and widespread period of racial harmony. With Powhatan's tribes now at peace with the English, the colony had only to mend relations with his more distant rivals or enemies. The Potomacs had earlier come to terms, as witnessed by their chief's betrayal of Pocahontas. It was time to bring the Chickahominies to heel, for they were "a lustie and daring people" with at least three hundred bowmen. The English could hardly afford their enmity. And again the rivalry of Indian tribes worked in Virginia's favor. Learning of the peace between the colony and Powhatan, the Chickahominies made speedy suit for a treaty of their own, lest the English back Powhatan who could then easily overwhelm them. The terms offered by the Chickahominies amounted to almost total sub-servience to the colony. As finally agreed between an English delegation under Dale and Argall on the one side, and the principal Chickahominy chiefs on the other, the tribe would henceforth be subject to King James and completely subordi-nate to his deputy in Virginia. Should the colony be attacked by Spain or by any Indians, the tribe would furnish it with three or four hundred bowmen. It would also prevent its own warriors from damaging English property and would pay annual tribute of two bushels of corn per man. In return the English pledged to provide the tribe with iron tomahawks, to defend it from Powhatan and other enemies, and to allow it local rule through its own laws and leaders. The English negotiators also promised a red coat annually to the eight members of the tribal council and a copper medallion en-graved with the King's picture, to be worn about the neck as a sign that they were "King James his noble men." Thereafter the tribe would be known by "the name of Tassantasses or English men." The Chickahominies, Hamor believed, pre-ferred "to be made one people with us, to curbe the pride and ambition of *Powhatan*. . . ."

The treaties that followed the Rolfe-Pocahontas marriage had advantages to the English besides the absence of warfare. The tribute in corn, combined with increasingly substantial English harvests, gave the colony its first adequate food sup-ply; thereafter the Indians, rather than the white men, had to importune their neighbors for corn. According to Samuel Purchas, this raised the Indians' regard for the colonists who had earlier been held "in base esteeme" for not being able to feed themselves. It also made possible a rapid enlargement of English landholdings, as lesser chiefs mortgaged their terri-tories for colonial grain. Surely some of those mortgages were eventually foreclosed. The colonists acquired further land when the Indians substituted acreage for corn in barters with the English; the Indians, with a superabundance of land, used it to acquire iron tools, cloth, and trinkets from the settlers.

Other sales may have reflected a realization that the English would soon control the area anyway, since the white men seemed determined to increase and expand. That determination looked more and more probable now that peace and security for the English had come at last, with (in the words of John Rolfe), "everie man [now] sitting under his *figtree* in safety."

A Declaration for the certaine time of dravving the great standing Lottery.

A broadside, appearing in London in 1615,
announces a lottery to aid Virginia.

VI
Search for Stability:
Economics

THE LONDON COMPANY as well as its colony sought
benefits from the Rolfe-Pocahontas marriage. Here was proof
that racial troubles had ended, that Indians could be converted, that a new day had dawned in British America. If
properly publicized, the marriage might also stimulate new
investments and new attempts to create a viable colonial
economy. With Indian attacks over at last, the colony could
renew its efforts to produce wine, silk, glass, and other exports.
Most experiments, however, required aid from the company,
which in turn depended on a favorable public image.

To that end, the company sponsored a brief home leave for
John Rolfe, Pocahontas ("his new convert and consort"), and
their infant son, Thomas, named for Governor Dale. On 12
June 1616, *Treasurer* docked in Plymouth, carrying among its
passengers Sir Thomas Dale, the Rolfes, and perhaps a dozen
Indians, including Tomocomo, one of Powhatan's councillors.
England greeted them cordially: crowds formed wherever the
Indian princess went; the Bishop of London entertained her
"with festivall state and pompe"; and Lord and Lady de la
Warr presented Rebecca, as Mistress Rolfe was now called, to
the royal court. Early in 1617 John Chamberlain reported to a
friend that "the Virginian woman . . . hath been with the
King and [was] graciously used, and both she and her assis-

tant well placed at the maske" — on this occasion a play by Ben Jonson. For almost a year, Pocahontas was the toast of London. The company's plan seemed successful.

Perhaps more important to Pocahontas than public acclaim was her first meeting with John Smith since his departure from Virginia seven years before. He had by no means forgotten her. He had already contributed to her reputation by writing a "little booke" about her to Queen Anne — although characteristically it said more about the captain than about his Indian friend, relating once again his escapades in Virginia and her timely aid. Smith lauded Pocahontas as "the first Christian ever of that Nation, the first *Virginian* ever spake *English,* or had a childe in mariage by an *Englishman,*" and urged the Queen to show her some special honor.

Smith met briefly with Pocahontas at Brentford near London, in a scene that must have touched them both deeply. Pocahontas had long thought him dead; not until she reached Plymouth did she learn otherwise. For her it was a reunion with a much beloved older friend. For Smith the meeting was equally poignant. The young lass who had helped him so often and whose presence had frequently added the only touch of gaiety to Jamestown during those early bitter years now stood before him a mature and accomplished woman. Smith would cherish this moment for the rest of his life.

Except for a few subsequent visits tò introduce her to "divers Courtiers and others, my acquaintances," Smith apparently did not see Pocahontas again. His activities on behalf of British America kept him well occupied throughout her stay in England. He could not, however, have avoided hearing news of her from time to time, nor of learning with deep sadness of her death just as she began the long voyage back to Virginia. She had been in England less than a year and had made a very favorable impression. But her health suffered badly, and shortly after boarding the *George* in London she had to be put ashore at the nearby Thames River port of Gravesend. There, as Smith recorded several years later in his *Generall Historie,* "it pleased God . . . to take this young Lady to his mercie." The Gravesend parish register records that on 21 March 1617, "Rebecca Wrolfe wyffe to Thomas [rather John] Wrolfe gent., A Virginia lady borne was buried in the chauncall." Leaving his son in the care of an uncle, John Rolfe set sail for Virginia to resume his duties as secretary of the resident council.

The years since his departure from Jamestown had been frustrating for John Smith. Without major employment and at perpetual odds with the officers of the London Company, Smith viewed Virginia's affairs with some bitterness. Still, he remained the colony's principal historian: his *Map of Virginia with a Description of the Countrey* (1612) provided the most detailed description yet published of the events since 1606, fuller even than the company's official publications, and more extensive than his own *True Relation* of 1608. It included too, as its title promised, a map of eastern Virginia, drawn from sketches he had made there, and which, along with his subsequent map of New England, would serve for many years as the principal cartographic work on British America. In 1616 came his third publication, *A Description of New England,* in which Smith told of the area that in recent years had attracted much of his time and energy. This book, like his earlier publications, combined first-hand accounts, edited versions of other men's reports, and remarkably accurate visual representation of the coastline and principal ports. And in keeping with literary fashion Smith included several testimonials, doggerel rhymes for the most part, to his own contribution as a colonist and explorer.

Unlike Smith's other works, both before and after 1616, *A Description of New England* avoided any important mention of the southern colony. Since about 1612 he had focused his sights on northern Virginia, as Englishmen called the area above the 41st parallel until John Smith named it "New England." None of the London and Plymouth Company records for this period survive, and Smith himself makes little mention of his own activities during these years, but he and the London Company probably were no longer amicable. Outspoken to a fault, Smith would hardly have been reticent about his opinion of the company's efforts in Virginia. Its leaders, on the other hand, were socially and politically prominent; they resented criticism from a yeoman's upstart son, no matter how many Turks and Indians he had slain. Whatever rebuffs he received from the company did not, however, deter the captain's determination to foster English colonization. The New World was in his blood now. He had caught a glimpse of the potentialities of British colonies in America, and for the rest of his life his vocations and avocations focused on the Atlantic seaboard. In the long run, he would give most of his loyalty and energy to the London Company's colony of Virginia, but for several years Smith cast his lot with the Plymouth group.

Until 1616 little had been done in the Plymouth Company's territory. Back in 1607 George Popham and Ralegh Gilbert had established a foothold on the Sagadohoc River in Maine, only to abandon it less than a year later when a series of tragedies brought a sudden collapse to promising beginnings. It had, among other misfortunes, lost a ship to Spanish patrols — a grim reminder that the Jamestown colony's wariness of Spain rested on fact. Because this early failure discouraged investors, and because the financial resources of the western counties did not match those of London, there was little activity in northern Virginia for the next seven years. John Smith became interested in the area sometime after 1612. "I liked *Virginia* well," he later wrote, "though not their proceedings; so I desired also to see this country, and spend some time in trying what I could finde. . . ."

He found something of lasting value. During a brief voyage to New England in 1614, Smith discovered — or rather publicized far more than anyone else — the very lucrative codfish, which he predicted would make settlement of the northern coast highly profitable. He also found sassafras in great quantities and other products that he believed would, in the long run, be as valuable as silver and gold. Smith discovered too a number of excellent ports and, drawing upon an earlier penchant, gave place names to every significant geographical location or feature he encountered. At least he proposed the names. He wisely saved the official designating for fifteen-year-old Prince Charles, whom Smith managed to approach through the good offices of his friend Robert Bertie, now Lord Willoughby. Smith's designations for some of the locations never caught hold, and many of his labels were later changed, but largely as a result of John Smith's explorations and cartography, New England itself received a permanent name.

Because of his important contributions to New England's reputation and because of his energetic explorations of the region, the Plymouth Company made Smith its "Admiral of New England." Such an honor should have led to repeated voyages to America and to a fairly generous income. Neither happened. Ill-luck plagued his efforts to plant a colony. In the summer of 1615 French pirates intercepted his second attempt to reach New England and held him prisoner while his own crew "ran away with my Ship and all that I had." For several months Smith was again a captive. He used the time well, however, drafting the *Description of New England*. In November 1615, he escaped in a harrowing episode that almost cost his life, and with timely aid from still another of his women saviors, one "Madame Chanoyes" of La Rochelle, made his way home to England. In 1617 Admiral Smith once more failed to reach New England when a fierce Atlantic storm pinned him for three months against the coast of England. By then the Plymouth Company's financial plight precluded further expeditions. In 1620 the company relinquished its charter; that same year a new organization, the Council for New England, secured rights to the northern part of the American coast. More concerned with parcelling New England into feudal fiefs than with exploiting its commercial possibilities, the new patentees had no use for John Smith.

In the halcyon days before his wife's death, John Rolfe had tried one of John Smith's favorite pastimes, writing promotional literature. Rolfe penned a *True Relation of the State of Virginia* during the visit to England; it was published, with many alterations, by Samuel Purchas in 1617. A year before the London Company had printed its latest *Briefe Declaration of the present state of things* (1616), and in 1617 it issued a broadside. All three publications had the same purpose: the rehabilitation of the colony's sagging reputation in hope of encouraging new investments. In those years, as in every year since the founding of the company a decade earlier, financial dilemmas threatened to end England's efforts at New World colonization. Too few adventurers would risk their money in an enterprise that insatiably consumed the company's meager resources and returned no salable cargo. Something new was needed to salvage the company's finances. John Rolfe's marriage had helped matters somewhat; his pamphlets contributed too. More important than either was his solution to the shortage of colonial exports.

Like many of his countrymen, Rolfe enjoyed puffing a pipe of tobacco, a taste that had caught hold rapidly in England after 1565 when John Hawkins brought some leaves from Florida. The habit had spread through the British Isles as it had throughout the world, and soon a small domestic production emerged. But tobacco did not flourish in the soil and climate of Britain. Englishmen would have to purchase their tobacco from Spanish America, a source they preferred to avoid, or grow an adequate supply in their own colony. Yet the harsh *nicotiana rustica* of the Virginia Indians could not compete with Spanish tobacco. As an early colonist complained, the Virginia leaf "is not of the best kynd, yt is but poore and weake, and of a byting tast." Rolfe provided a simple answer: import seeds from Trinidad and the Orinoco River Valley, where the best varieties grow, and plant them in Virginia's willing soil.

Rolfe planted those seeds in 1611. A year later he had his first crop: in another year he had enough to export, though barely a sample. Despite its continuing inferiority to Spanish leaves (because of the Virginians' inexperience with curing techniques) Rolfe's brand far surpassed the native product and found a ready market in England. In 1615 the colony sent home more than 2000 lbs., a figure that jumped tenfold in the next two years. It rose to 40,000 lbs. in 1620, to 60,000 in 1622, to 500,000 in 1626, and to 1,500,000 in 1629, when it leveled off until the end of the century. Variations in harvests, English commercial policies, and international competition caused prices to fluctuate wildly. In the early decades the price hovered near three pence a pound, promising a healthy return to Virginia growers and, potentially at least, a profit for English investors.

Virginia went tobacco mad. In 1614 the first settlers' terms of seven years labor for the company ended; as prospective freeholders they could soon do with their own land as they pleased. And they pleased to sow tobacco. So did the other settlers, for in 1614 acting-governor Dale leased to each adult male three acres of "cleere corne ground" on which to grow his family's subsistence. At first all went well and food became plentiful. There was, however, little market for corn in Virginia and no demand for it in England. The settlers therefore switched to tobacco and almost totally neglected less lucrative but essential food crops. By 1617 John Rolfe was complaining that, given a chance, the colonists would "spend too much of their tyme and labor in planting *Tobacco,* knowen to them to be verie vendible in England, and so neglect their tillage of Corne. . . ." In an effort to keep Virginia's economy stable through a diversity of products, Dale decreed that no one could grow tobacco unless he also planted two acres of corn for himself and each male servant, at pain of forfeiting all his tobacco to the colony.

Dale's regulation helped to make corn plentiful again, but the urge for quick profits spurred every planter to grow as much tobacco as he could. Returns seemed to justify the effort. In 1619 a man working by himself could raise tobacco worth £200 sterling; with the help of six servants, if he could find that many, he could earn £1000. Secretary of the colony John Pory complained that "all our riches for the present doe consiste in Tobacco." But the riches depended more on quantity than on quality, and they depended on more laborers than the colony had. In their hurry to share the sudden wealth, many farmers set more plants than they could tend; failure to remove some of the leaves on each stalk produced such an inferior quality that London tobacco mongers began to call their trash tobacco "Virginian."

The mania for tobacco disturbed the leaders in England who cared about the future of Virginia, especially King James. As early as 1604 he had so strongly objected to the "noxious weed" that he issued *A Counter Blaste to Tobacco*. In that famous diatribe the King, with uncanny foresight, attacked smoking as "a custome lothsome to the eye, hatefull to the Nose, harmefull to the braine, daungerous to the Lungs, and in the blacke stinking fume thereof, neerest resembling the horrible Stigian smoke of the pit that is bottomelesse." James Stuart's antipathy for tobacco lay only partly in its danger to the user and annoyance to the non-smoker. He also feared that unrestrained raising of tobacco precluded the development of crops less dramatic but more important to the welfare of the empire. The King wanted his American colony to provide commodities that would otherwise have to come from Europe or Asia, and he believed Virginia admirably suited for such a task. Her southerly latitude suggested that she could produce the silk, wine, and citrus fruits that came from Mediterranean countries. Her tall stands of timber promised the masts, spars, pitch, and tar that came from Russia, Poland, and Scandinavia. Her many and varied fur-bearing animals assured England of the pelts then purchased from Baltic nations. Other natural products of Virginia included hemp, salt, dyes, medicinal drugs, sugar cane, cotton, and especially iron. If properly exploited, Virginia could become more valuable than all the gold mines of Spanish America.

James gave special attention to silk and wine. In 1622 the King commanded silk works to be set up and vines planted in lieu of tobacco. He even sent to Virginia two shipments of silkworms from his royal nursery. They failed to survive the voyage, and in spite of royal concern and considerable expense by the company, silk never flourished in English America. The effort persisted, however. John Bonoeil, a Frenchman whom the company considered an expert on silk and other agricultural matters, wrote two detailed treatises to help Virginians set up the necessary facilities. His first effort, in 1620, explained how to plant mulberry trees, of which Virginia had good supply, and how to produce ample numbers of worms. "In the Spring time," Bonoeil advised, "shut up a young Calfe in a little darke and dry stable, and there feed it onely with Mulbery leaves some twenty dayes. . . . At the end of this time, kill it by strangling, and put it whole into a tub, to rot there, and cover it all over with Mulbery leaves: out of the corruption of this carcase, come forth abundance of Silkwormes. . . ." The failure of Virginia's silk works may owe a good deal to this pseudo-scientific Frenchman. Undaunted, in 1622 Bonoeil issued a second treatise, prefaced by an admonition from the King to get on with the project, and an afterword from the treasurer of the company directing each Virginia settler to plant vines and mulberry trees in accordance with "his Majesties Royall Commands." The company sent a copy of Bonoeil's book to every head of a family, so they might learn not only how to produce silk and wine, and make silkworm houses "in forme of a Bowling Alley," but also how to grow most kinds of fruit trees, including fig, olive, and pomegranate. A small quantity of wine, of poor quality, eventually reached England. The other ventures produced nothing.

In the end, of course, victory went to the "smoakie Witch." In 1624 Governor Harvey decried "the immoderate plantinge of tobacco," yet he too was powerless to stop it. By that time even the Crown had given up the fight.

Tobacco might not please the King, but tobacco revenue pleased him very much. To help the colony and to secure as much income as possible from this tawdry source, the Crown gave Virginia and Bermuda a monopoly on tobacco by prohibiting its growth in the British Isles and excluding or strictly limiting all foreign imports. In return, James insisted, all tobacco had to enter through a customs house in London where after 1619 it incurred a substantial duty. The King would allow tobacco production only "untill by more solid Commodityes they be able to substitute otherwise"; in the meantime he wanted no evasion of duties. When widespread smuggling and other subterfuges became rampant, the King contracted with private agents to receive and grade all tobacco in return for a fixed payment to the Crown. The contractors made handsome profits at the expense of the planters, touching off a tedious squabble over how best to ship and market the commodity. But despite frequent changes in regulations and shifts in market prices, tobacco had come to Virginia to stay. For all its faults it accomplished what no other crop had done: it brought a measure of prosperity to the impoverished colony. That prosperity had not come the way John Smith had envisioned, nor the way the company's council or the King had wanted, but in its attempt to carve profitable colonies out of the wilderness, England could not be choosy.

By 1616, when Dale and the Rolfes set sail for England, some stability had come to the colonial enterprise. Government, though harsh, was at least orderly, and based for the first time on published regulations. Thanks to tobacco, Virginia's economic situation showed more promise than at any time since the founding of Jamestown, even though substantial profits were largely in the future and were already dominated by a handful of influential men. Relations with the Indians, though still based largely on *force majeure* rather than true understanding and partnership between Indians and Englishmen, had reached a peaceful plateau after years of bloodshed. Not without reason did both colonists and company seize on these good omens to predict that Virginia's troubles had ended.

The colony's new prosperity was reflected in its physical dispersal. Whereas Jamestown and Point Comfort had long monopolized Virginia's settlement, by 1616 four new plantations had been established — Henrico, Bermuda Hundred, West and Shirley Hundred, and Dale's Gift. Thirty-eight men and boys, most of them farmers, lived at Henrico, fifteen miles below the falls of the James River. Bermuda Hundred, on the south side of the James about five miles below Henrico, housed one hundred nineteen settlers, most of them working on potash, tar, and charcoal as well as the usual agricultural crops. Across the river about twenty-five lived at West and Shirley Hundred, mostly engaged in tobacco farming, while at the mouth of Chesapeake Bay near Cape Charles, seventeen men caught fish and made salt for the colony. Twenty settlers, half of them farmers, resided at the older settlement of Kecoughtan near Point Comfort, and fifty colonists still lived on Jamestown peninsula, which had shed much of its reputation for unhealthiness. In 1614 Jamestown boasted "two faire rowes of howses, all of framed Timber, two stories, and an upper Garret, or Corne loft," in addition to several substantial storehouses and fortifications. Deputy Governor George Yeardley resided at Bermuda Hundred, as did Alexander Whitaker, "sonn to that reverend and famous *Divine Doctor Whitaker*." Reverend William Wickham ministered to the flock at Henrico, and William Mays performed the same services at Kecoughtan.

In keeping with the new emphasis on order and stability, the settlers had been divided into three comprehensive categories: officers, laborers, and farmers. The officers, drawn almost exclusively from the gentry, commanded the other two categories in both civilian and military duties. Two kinds of laborers served under them — those who worked for the company and received their maintenance at public expense, and those who worked for and supported themselves. Most of the former were unskilled, the latter largely craftsmen. According to John Rolfe, the farmers lived "at most ease." Except for annual taxes of two and one half barrels of corn, thirty-one days of public labor, and occasional turns at watch and ward, the farmer enjoyed considerable freedom. And with fifty or more acres of fertile ground he could, if he had ambition, live well. In Henrico the farmer might have one of the new timber and brick houses, on a par with the better English houses; he might purchase "all manner of clothing, household stuff and such necessaries" at the company magazine at reasonable rates; and he might own several of the 216 goats, 144 head of cattle, and 6 horses reported in Virginia in 1616. (Both wild and tame hogs were so plentiful as "not to be nombred," a striking change since the starving time of six years before.) There appeared at last to be some substance to the lavish claims, made frequently and sometimes too enthusiastically by friends of English colonization, that in Virginia England had an earthly paradise. Perhaps, in fact, she did, especially if one could believe Sir Thomas Dale's judgment that thanks to "the blessing of God and good government," the colony had recovered from its earlier ill times.

That judgment, however, reflected Dale's assessment of the colony in 1616, the year of his departure. So did John Rolfe's subsequent contention that Virginia's former condition had "somewhat bettered, for we have sufficient to content our selves, though not in such abundance as is vainly reported in *England*." Rolfe had no business complaining of false reports for he had been one of the principal propagandists during his recent visit to England. Yet his point was valid. Despite nine years of intensive effort, England still had not solved the dilemmas of colonization. The cost in lives and pounds sterling remained high. And although conditions had improved appreciably during the previous decade, Virginia fell far short of everyone's expectations.

Rolfe discovered how fast the colony could deteriorate on his return there in 1617. He found Jamestown in near ruin, with only five or six houses habitable, the church down, the palisades broken, the wharf in pieces, and the well spoiled. "The Store-house they used for the Church; the market-place, and streets, and all other spare places [were] planted with Tobacco." The rest of the colony fared little better, and of the four hundred settlers he considered "not past 200 fit for husbandry and tillage." Dale's successor as deputy-governor, Samuel Argall, with whom Rolfe returned to Virginia, tried to remedy this latest wave of disorder, but even the elements thwarted him. A severe drought and a violent hail storm destroyed much of the harvest of 1618, while adverse winds forced the *George* to waste five months crossing the Atlantic with supplies. By the time the ship arrived, most of its provisions had spoiled. To meet this new crisis, the company dispatched a larger and better stocked ship with two hundred new colonists under the command of Governor de la Warr, who was still nominally in charge of the colony but still suffering from the ailments that had kept him in England since 1612. Adverse winds caught this ship too, and during the troubled voyage of almost four months, disease struck. Thirty passengers, including Lord de la Warr, died at sea.

News of the governor's death and reports that additional ships would soon dock with more mouths to feed devastated the colony, still reeling from shortages caused by bad weather and the arrival of two vessels in deplorable condition. History, it appeared, repeated itself inexorably in Virginia: hope, despair, renewed hope, renewed and more bitter despair. The cycle seemed endless.

Time and again the colony's problems reflected the company's poverty. Successful colonization, it became increasingly apparent, cost colossal sums of money; Virginia represented a bottomless pit, forever absorbing the stockholders' funds without a pence of profit. And so, while the early colonists struggled to survive Indian attacks and malnutrition, the company's leaders groped for fiscal solvency. With adequate funds they could supply the colony until it became self-supporting; an empty treasury threatened disaster to settlers and promoters alike.

In 1616 the London Company launched an imaginative drive to tap new sources of income. By convincing the Crown to permit lotteries, common in Europe and of growing popularity in England, the company hoped to attract investments from Englishmen who cared nothing for Virginia but who could not resist a game of chance. A new royal charter, issued early in 1612, included authorization, and plans were immediately laid for a drawing. For prizes the company offered not wilderness but cash or its equivalent, to be provided from the funds raised by the lottery itself.

The "First Great Standing Lottery" for Virginia was encouraging. Announced early in 1612, the drawing took place that summer; a London tailor named Thomas Sharplisse won the top prize of a thousand pounds "in fayre plate, which was sent to his house in a very stately manner." The company apparently realized a profit of several thousand pounds. Another grand lottery and two lesser lotteries began at once. The smaller ones did poorly, despite a modest price of 12d per ticket, partly because of low public confidence stemming from fraudulent management and partly because of "some lewd aspertions that no good successe was likely." Contributions remained so sparse that the company twice postponed the drawing.

The second grand lottery, which opened in the summer of 1612, had more success, but only after inauspicious beginnings. Perhaps because of their five shilling price, the tickets sold slowly and the drawing had to be delayed. Complaining that "the adventurers came in so slackly with such poore and barren receits of moneys," the company sought help from the Privy Council. That body ordered copies of an illustrated broadside, with covering endorsement, sent to every city, town, and county in England. This "Great standing Lotterie," the broadside promised, would be the last chance to aid a worthy cause and perhaps to strike it rich in the process. The prizes must have looked attractive to anyone with a few shillings to spare: a "Great Prize" of nearly £1200, two second prizes of £500 each, and 9,700 other cash awards. In addition the lottery offered "Welcomes & Rewards." "To him that first shall bee drawne out with a Blank" would go a welcome of £25; "To him that putteth in the greatest number of Lots under one name" would go a reward of £100, and so on to more than a score of supplementary awards. The grand total of cash prizes offered by the company came to almost £25,000, in amounts ranging from ten shillings to £1125.

To distribute such a sum and have enough left over to finance expeditions to Virginia, the London Company had to sell an extraordinary number of tickets. Solicitations to the cities, towns, and counties helped, as did a similar appeal to the craft and merchant companies of London and a separate endorsement to the companies by the Lord Mayor. Helpful too, perhaps, was a ditty, sung to the tune of "Lusty Gallant," that urged prospective buyers to:

> Let no man thinke that he shall loose,
> > though he no Prize poscesse:
> His substaunce to Virginia goes,
> > which God, no doubt will blesse:
> And in short time send from that land,
> > much rich commoditie;
> So shall we thinke all well bestowd,
> > upon this Lotterie.

In a more pragmatic vein, the company encouraged investors by offering membership to anyone who contributed £12.10 to the lottery, provided he relinquish his prizes, and anyone who owed money to the company could have his debts forgiven without jeopardizing his winnings by investing double the amount in the lottery. Finally, "to hasten the drawing of our Lottery, as chiefly to enable us the sooner to make good supplies to the Colonie in Virginia," anyone who adventured £3 "ready money" would be given a silver spoon worth 6s 8d or that amount in cash. Still, contributions lagged, and not until November 17, 1615, did the drawing begin at the company's lottery house in the west end of St. Paul's churchyard. In the absence of company records little is known about the outcome. Presumably the company realized a profit, but not great enough to justify additional lotteries of the same sort.

Although it held no more standing lotteries in London, between 1616 and 1620 the Virginia Company conducted, through hired agents, several smaller "running lotteries" throughout rural England. With frequent drawings and scrupulous management, the running lotteries enjoyed remarkable popularity as they moved from town to town across Britain, confirming the opinion of one agent that "smale Townes & greate markettes doth exceed the best Citties. . . ." Despite occasional suspicions of fraud, the lotteries were the principal source of company income from 1612 to 1621, when the Crown, under pressure from Parliament, withdrew the organization's authority to conduct such events. No precise figures survive, but scraps of evidence suggest that the net total could have reached forty or fifty thousand pounds — nearly half the company's income during the nine years of the lotteries' existence. The lotteries had truly been, as a member of the company observed, "the reall and substantial food by which Virginia hath been nourished."

Well aware that lottery profits could not by themselves underwrite colonization, the company launched another scheme for swelling its coffers and at the same time increasing the flow of permanent settlers to Virginia. The London Company held one tangible asset of great appeal to all Englishmen: land. Some of it would soon be assigned to the original settlers and stockholders, but a vast amount remained the property of the corporation. In 1616 the company voted to offer fifty-acre tracts to anyone who went to Virginia at his own expense or who bought a full share of stock at £12.10; if they began payment before 25 June 1616, they would be eligible for all benefits "as if with the Old Adventurers they had been partakers from the beginning." To encourage investors of moderate means, a broadside announced that new stockholders could pay half the cost at once, the rest in six months. Each stockholder would receive a fifty-acre plot along the James River or around the inland towns and would receive additional plots as later dividends occurred. The total grant per man might reach 200 acres — a fabulous estate for a seventeenth-century Englishman. In 1617 the company expanded its land policy by granting fifty acres at each division to anyone who paid another's passage to the colony. Through such "headrights" the company gained doubly: it avoided the heavy costs of shipping men and women to America, and it acquired common laborers who could not pay their own way. Although a labor shortage plagued Virginia throughout the seventeenth century, the headright system abated it appreciably.

So did another major innovation introduced at the same time. With the initial distribution in 1616 of the company's land, several large stockholders received vast tracts. This, however, raised questions of jurisdiction and organization: could the proprietor, like the lord of an English manor, enjoy traditional rights and privileges over the tenants to whom he rented his soil? Could several landholders pool their holdings, form a subcompany to develop their land, and regulate the laborers they sent to it? And would the London Company encourage this kind of settlement in the hope that it would promote more rapid colonization at no expense to the other stockholders?

Indeed it would. The company had much to gain and very little to lose by letting one or more stockholders finance "particular plantations." There lingered the danger that jurisdictional squabbles might arise between the resident government and agents of a private plantation (which happened occasionally), or that the plantations would raise tobacco to the total exclusion of all other products (which happened often). But the company held a trump it could always play: by royal grant the London Company alone held jurisdiction over the area within its assigned boundaries. It could therefore set any stipulation it wanted in issuing subcharters and could revoke them in cases of dispute. And because most patentees would themselves be experienced members of the company, difficulties could probably be worked out within the parent organization itself.

Precedents for creating subsidiaries abounded. Much English exploration and settlement had been underwritten by investors who contributed to a single project in return for a proportional share of the profits, and on the whole the scheme had worked well. As early as 1608, for example, a London goldsmith named Richard Widdows had contributed £25 to a supply ship going to Virginia, in return for a share of the land, precious metals, pearls, and stones "or any kinde of wares or Merchandizes, commodities or profits whatsoever which shall be obtayned or gotten in the said voyage. . . ." Many other expeditions had been financed by particular rather than general joint-stocks. Furthermore, Bermuda had from the outset been settled on a pattern of quasi-independent "tribes" or parishes, each under the proprietorship of an individual investor or association of several investors. And since most Bermuda stockholders were also members of the Virginia Company, the policies were easily transferred from the newer organization to the older. The relative success of Bermuda enhanced the possibility of such transfer. In 1616 the islands' population stood at almost 600, Virginia's at only 350. Sometime in 1617 or 1618 the London Company granted to Sir

Edwin Sandys and associates a patent for land that eventually became known as Southampton's Hundred, and another to John Smyth of Nibley and his associates for land that became Berkeley Hundred. Similar grants followed. For the next several years many of the passengers and goods on most ships to Virginia went under the auspices of particular plantations. Largely through the efforts of the new patentees, Virginia's population jumped from less than 400 in 1617 to 1000 in early 1619, and to nearly 3500 in 1622.

With its economic well-being considerably improved, the London Company turned to other matters. For several years a growing faction had urged more effective policies and a more vigorous administration. Eventually the reformers got their chance; the pressure they brought to bear on the company's leaders resulted in several far-reaching measures. It also led to still another change in the colony's leadership.

In 1618 the company selected George Yeardley to succeed Samuel Argall. Argall's abundant faults included an inability to separate his public and private investments, for as acting governor of the colony and a major stockholder in a plantation he encountered a conflict of interest that his critics insisted he too often decided in favor of his personal affairs. Yeardley, a veteran of war in the Netherlands, a survivor of the shipwreck on Bermuda, and acting governor between Dale's departure with the Rolfes in 1616 and Argall's arrival in 1617, had solid qualifications for the job. Like Argall, he had to juggle commitments to the colony and to a particular plantation, but the new governor had considerably more integrity. And Yeardley's most obvious shortcoming, his lack of a title, was soon remedied by a knighthood. That turned Yeardley's head for the moment. John Chamberlain gossiped to Sir Dudley Carleton that the honor "hath set him up so high that he flaunts yt up and downe the streets in extraordinarie braverie, with fourteen or fifteen fayre liveries after him." No matter; Sir George had little time to show off. He was appointed governor in November, 1618, and arrived in Virginia the following April.

Under Yeardley the company tried "to Ease all the Inhabitants of Virginia forever of all taxes and public burthens as much as may be and to take away all occasion of oppression and corruption." It set aside several three-thousand-acre plots for support of the colony, to be worked by tenants sent for that purpose — half their labor going to the maintenance of the colonial officers, half to themselves. The "tenants-at-halves" would thus be self-sufficient yet would relieve most of the need for taxes. Additional revenue would accrue from rent of one shilling per year on every fifty acres allotted to settlers arriving after 1616 and on lands of pre-1616 settlers who had come at company expense. Employees of the London Company sent to Virginia after 1616 were to serve seven years before gaining a share of land; in the meantime they would live as tenants-at-halves on company land at Charles City, Henrico, Kecoughtan, or Jamestown.

The London Company also encouraged local government by assigning to each borough, including particular plantations, fifteen hundred acres to support its officials. And with an eye to the colony's social needs, it allotted one hundred acres to each community as glebe land and ten thousand acres at Henrico to support public education. Such a generous land policy encouraged a fresh flood of immigrants. But land policies were only a start. The company had other, more basic, reforms in mind.

A conjectural drawing of Jamestown and vicinity about 1618

VII
Reform

Since the founding of Virginia in 1607 it had become increasingly clear that the colony could not depend entirely on the decisions made in far-away England by men who had for the most part never set eyes on America. Yeardley no doubt felt this strongly, having worked for the company on both sides of the Atlantic; he, de la Warr, Gates, and others may have encouraged the creation of a Virginia assembly to make laws for the colony and to act as its highest court. It is likely, too, that Captain John Smith added his voice to such a chorus. He had never approved of the company's absentee rulership and had often vented his contempt for London's rich and pompous armchair explorers; any scheme that increased the authority of the colonists at the expense of the company could not be all bad. The company would not, of course, have directly solicited Smith's advice; his impact on the decision to establish an American assembly came from his writings and from the private opinions he conveyed to Samuel Purchas and other friends of English colonization.

Some years earlier the company had cared little about the colonists' views on government or anything else. At that stage Virginia had been quasi-military in form and function. By 1619 a profound transformation was underway. The colony had become a predominantly agricultural community of independent farmers, each with his own land and equipment, many with wives and children. As threats of Indian and Spanish attack dwindled and as economic prospects brightened, the burgeoning population spread into a dozen scattered communities. The company responded with new political and judicial forms. It established monthly courts in the outlying precincts (revamped in 1634 into shire or county courts) for petty crimes, and in 1619 it devised a colonial assembly to promote cohesion among the dispersed plantations, to act as a superior court, and to encourage mutual responsibility. As the Bermuda Company observed when it fashioned a similar body the next year, "every man will more willingly obey lawes to which he hath yeilded his consent."

The London Company viewed the representative assembly as a moderate and pragmatic innovation. In the mother country every man with a freehold income of forty shillings per year — evidence that he had "a stake in society" — could vote for delegates to the House of Commons. In land-rich Virginia all freemen had that much property and were thus entitled to political participation. (John Smith discerningly referred to the first Assembly as "Their time of Parlament.") Furthermore, the free settlers were stockholders in the London Company by virtue of having adventured their persons instead of their money, and of course some had done both. They had no voice in the company, however, unless they happened to be in London during a quarterly meeting of the "General Court." A resident assembly would give the settlers a parallel legislative body. And in any event, the company had given up none of its real authority. All decisions of the Assembly required ratification in London, and the company's power to appoint and remove the governor (who retained a veto over the Assembly) and to issue his instructions, remained absolute. Even the company's promise to delay future regulations from London until they had been approved by the colonial assembly was freely given and could as freely be taken away.

Governor Yeardley's instructions did not mention the Assembly, the most significant reform of 1618–1619. Presumably a separate "Great Charter," which has since been lost but its substance preserved in a similar document of 1621, authorized a body consisting of the governor, his council, and two representatives from each town or particular plantation. The free inhabitants or "burgesses" had the privilege of selecting their delegates; the franchise qualifications are not known, but probably every adult male not serving under an indenture could vote. The General Assembly was to meet "yearly of Course & no oftener but for very extreordynarie & Important occasions"; it would attend to all matters "concerning the puplique weale" and "make ordeine & enact such generall lawes & orders" as good government required. Later in the century the representatives became a separate body, styled the "House of Burgesses," in a bicameral legislature.

The value of a resident legislature became clear at its first session. On 25 June 1619, Yeardley called for elections; on 30 July twenty-two burgesses from eleven constituencies convened in the Jamestown church along with the six members of the council (among them John Rolfe) and Governor Yeardley. "The most convenient place we could finde to sitt," reported secretary John Pory, "was the quire of the Churche." Yeardley took his regular seat of honor, with the council on either side of him and Pory, now elected speaker, in front. After a prayer by Reverend Bucke asking "God to guide us & sanctifie all our proceedings to his owne glory, and the good of this Plantation," the burgesses took the Oath of Supremacy and were officially installed as members of the Assembly.

Four representatives faced challenges to seats, two from Captain Warde's plantation and two from Captain Martin's. Both cases reflected the problems of supervising particular plantations. Although Warde had settled without a patent from the company, the Assembly seated his delegation (which included Warde himself) because the captain had proved a devoted and helpful colonist and because he gave assurance that he would secure a clear title before the next meeting of the Assembly. Martin's delegation, on the other hand, failed to be seated even though he had a *bona fide* patent because it specifically exempted him "from any commaunde of the Colony, excepte it be in ayding & assisting the same against any forren or domestical Enemy." Martin's plantation thus formed a separate and autonomous community, linked to Virginia only through a mutual defense pact. The Assembly objected to letting his people help make laws that they were in no way bound to observe; Martin must relinquish the controversial clause in his patent or else his representatives "were utterly to be excluded, as being spies, rather than loyal Burgesses. . . ." Martin refused to budge, and so did the Assembly.

With matters of membership temporarily resolved, the first General Assembly labored for six days on a wide range of problems. True to English tradition, it concerned itself first with law. Which of the instructions given to de la Warr, Argall, and Yeardley, the Assembly had to decide, "might conveniently putt on the habite of Lawes," and what laws might be proposed "out of the private conceipte" of the burgesses? The statutes that emerged from their deliberations ran a gamut from setting the price of tobacco at three shillings per pound for best grade and eighteen pence for "the second sorte," to establishing penalties for servants who broke their terms of indenture. In between were laws against injury to Indians, idleness, gambling with cards or dice ("both winners & loosers shall forfaite ten shilling a man"), drunkenness, and "excess of apparell"; laws, too, for conversion of the Indians, raising silk, flax, hemp, and grape vines, and planting mulberry trees (a minimum of six per year for seven years by every land owner); and laws regulating tradesmen, servants, the company storehouse, travel, and more than a score of other matters.

In striking contrast to the earlier *Lawes Divine, Morall and Martiall*, the enactments of the General Assembly levied moderate penalties. Under Dale's Code anyone who killed a domestic or farm animal, even a hen of his own, without the governor's permission was to suffer death; accessories to the crime were to be burned on the hand and have both ears

cropped. Under the new laws, a similar offense merited forfei-
ture of the animal, nothing more. Another example: under
the Dale Code unauthorized absence from twice-daily divine
services cost the offender a day's allowance for the first offense,
a whipping for the second, and six months as a drudge for the
third. The laws of 1619 do not mention daily services; for each
absence from Sunday services an offender forfeited three shillings to the church. Only servants, with no funds of their own,
could receive corporal punishment. Draconian law had ended
in Virginia.

Before the Assembly adjourned on Wednesday, August 4,
because of "the intemperature of the Weather, & the falling
sicke of diverse of the Burgesses," the new body had accomplished a remarkable amount of constructive work. In addition to its legislative duties, the Assembly had acted as the
supreme judicial body of the colony, and in that capacity
meted out penalties for a variety of infractions. For the most
part it assigned lenient punishments although it occasionally
resorted to severity. A "lewd and trecherous servant" whose
alleged crimes included abusing his master, "wantonness"
with a woman servant, and false accusations, was condemned
to stand four days with his ears nailed to the pillory and be
whipped each day. Captain Henry Spelman, the young man
who had spent much of his life with the Indians and had been
saved by Pocahontas during the starving time, was indicted for
speaking disparagingly of Governor Yeardley to Opechancanough, thus bringing the Governor "in much disesteem both
with *Opochancano* & the Indians, & the whole Colony in
danger of their Slippery designes." Convinced that his crime
merited the death penalty, but unwilling to act on the basis of
a single witness, the court stripped Spelman of his title and
condemned him to seven years' service as the governor's interpreter. Unimpressed by this leniency, Spelman muttered some
uncomplimentary words which seemed to the recorder entirely
appropriate for "one that had in him more of the Savage then
of the Christian." Spelman might not be happy with his

plight, but he could at least take some comfort in knowing that he had been judged by his countrymen rather than by an arbitrary governor.

Of more immediate importance to the Virginia colonists was the General Assembly's ability to petition the London Company with good prospects of success. The Assembly urged the company to straighten out overlapping land grants; to send more tenants for the company lands and ministers' glebes, and workmen to erect college and university buildings; to give "old planters" grants in the second, third, and fourth distributions of land on a par with those of more recent planters; to grant a share of land to each male child, they "being the onely hope of a Posterity," and to wives "because that in a newe plantation it is not knowen whether man or woman be the most necessary"; and to permit collection of rents in commodities rather than money "whereof we have none at all, as we have no minte." While waiting for answers and for approval of the laws it had hurriedly passed, the Assembly put its decisions into effect, "for otherwise this people (who nowe at length have gott the raines of former servitude into their owne swindge) would in short time grow so insolent, as they would shake off all government, & there would be no living among them."

Nothing is known of the General Assembly of 1620. There may not have been one because the new wave of disease (typhoid, perhaps, or yellow fever) that had prematurely ended the first Assembly lingered on. The epidemic hit Englishmen and Indians alike, "to the consumption of divers hundreds, and almost the utter destruction of some particular *Plantations.*" Somehow the colony and the company, both inured to hardship, took this latest set-back in stride. The old planters now had land of their own, and in the words of a company broadside of 1621, the "sweetnesse of proprietie made them emulous to exceed each other in building and planting." Moreover, "the rigour of Martiall Law, wherewith before they were governed, is reduced within the limits prescribed by his Majesty," with the forms of government and justice "as neere as may be" to those in England. Once again the company's propaganda took liberties with the facts, but, rhetoric aside, the colonists could find cause for optimism in the knowledge that a vigorous and sympathetic administration now held sway in London.

For a decade following 1609 Sir Thomas Smythe served as treasurer of the London Company, at first with the almost unanimous support of his colleagues but increasingly with opposition. Disenchantment with his leadership soon found a spokesman in Sir Edwin Sandys. Long a member of the company and its inner circle of active stockholders, Sandys gradually lost confidence in Smythe's leadership and by 1617 began to build a faction against him. At least part of the resentment of Smythe stemmed from his casual handling of fiscal and other records — a charge borne out by subsequent investigations — and from a notable lack of success with both the investors' funds and the settlers' circumstances. And while there could be no doubt of Smythe's sincere interest in British imperialism — he simultaneously served as treasurer of the Virginia Company, governor of the East India Company, governor of the Muscovy Company, governor of the Northwest Passage Company, and governor of the Bermuda or Somers Island Company — he had clearly spread himself too thin to give Virginia the attention it needed.

Sandys' wing of the company differed from Smythe's not only in its determination to give undivided energy to the needs of Britain's American outpost, but also in its attitude toward change. Smythe had tinkered with details, for the most part, had changed leaders more than basic policies, and had left most important decisions in the hands of the colonial governor and his council. His few long-range efforts to revitalize the colony's political well-being had not been entirely successful — the *Lawes Divine, Morall and Martiall* are a case in point. And while Smythe could take pride in his attempts to salvage the company's sagging finances, some of which the new administration retained after it seized the helm, his reforms were too superficial and came too late. Sandys insisted on fundamental reforms, the sooner the better, and largely directed from London.

Late in 1618 the rift between the two factions came to a head. In the annual election the following spring, the dissidents elected Sir Edwin treasurer. Sir Thomas Smythe declined to run for office, perhaps to avoid an embarrassing defeat by Sandys, who had a reputation for clever and not always scrupulous maneuvering in Parliament. Smythe continued to head the Bermuda Company, and he and his followers remained major stockholders in the London Company, but his near-absolute power over the Jamestown experiment had ended. For the rest of the company's life, Sandys dominated its affairs. His tenure as treasurer was brief, however, for in 1620 King James strongly opposed his reelection. The King, John Chamberlain reported, "tooke greate exceptions to Sir Edwin Sands as [the] principall man that had withstoode him in Parliment and traducted his government. . . ." If Sandys could not be treasurer he could, nonetheless, secure the election of a man of his liking. In June 1620 the company chose the Earl of Southampton, Shakespeare's former patron and a prominent politician in his own right, who served for the next three years as a figurehead for Sandys.

The shift in leadership from Smythe to Sandys to Southampton did not slow the pace of reform. Sandys followed up Smythe's belated innovations with some of his own, especially a revision of the company's structure and rules. The charter of 1612, the company's third, had granted greater autonomy to the organization by vesting permanent authority in the stockholders' meetings. Yet no systematic restructuring of the company occurred until Sandys took office. He quickly brought order — at least on paper — to the unwieldy organization, and published the results in the hope that the public might regain some confidence in the Virginia project.

The "Orders and Constitutions, Partly collected out of his Majesties *Letters Patents*, and partly ordained upon mature deliberation, by the Treasuror, Counseil and Companie of Virginia" appeared in 1620 as an appendix to another promotional tract. Here the reader learned how the wheels of English colonization turned. He discovered, for example, that the power of decision now rested with the full membership of the company through four general or quarter courts, which alone had authority to select the company's officers and councillors as well as those of the colony, to make laws for both company and colony, to dispose of land in Virginia, and to make major decisions on matters of trade. Elections of the company's councillors and officers took place by secret ballot at the Easter term session; at that time the treasurer must report on the "estate of the *Colony*" as well as on the "present state of the Cash." No man could be elected treasurer who simultaneously held the governorship of any other company except the Bermuda Company — an obvious slur against Sir Thomas Smythe's multiple offices and evidence that the "Orders and Constitutions" reflected the policies of the Sandys administration rather than its predecessor. Also aimed at Smythe's excessively long tenure was a provision limiting the treasurer and deputy to three consecutive years in office. Councillors held office for life unless removed by the General Court, but they had to serve the company for at least a year prior to election and must be men of prestige and social standing: "None hereafter under the degree of a *Lord* or principall Magistrate, shall be chosen to be of his Majesties Counseil for *Virginia*."

Although most of the "Orders and Constitutions" concerned the London Company rather than the Virginia colony, the latter received some attention. Colony-wide officials now included the governor, lieutenant governor, admiral, marshall, chief justice, treasurer, and the resident councillors. All served at the company's pleasure, with a six-year limit for the governor, and to be supported by the public lands. Proprietors of particular plantations must henceforth be subordinate to the colonial officials and to its courts and General Assembly and must employ their tenants on commodities such as corn, wine, silk, iron, and clapboard, "and not wholly or chiefly about *Tabacco,* and *Sassaphras.*"

Under the tutelage of the Sandys-Southampton party, Virginia seemed to have shaken off the mistakes of the past. In 1617 John Rolfe had pointed out that during the first few years the colony had been ruled "by a *President & Councell Aristocratycallie*" under which "such envie, dissentions and jarrs were daily sowen amongst them, that they *choaked* the *seedes* and *blasted* the *fruits* of all mens labors." Then came the charter of 1609, under which "a more absolute government was graunted *Monarchally*. . . ." That had clearly failed too. Now, in the early 1620s, Samuel Purchas boasted that "both the Company here, and the Colony in Virginia, have their businesse carried regularly, industriously, and justly, every man knowing both his right and dutie. . . ." It would be too much to argue that Virginia had become a democracy, but elements of a democratic system existed where none had before. The colony had published laws in conformity with those of the mother country; a governor so restrained by a council that "he can doe wrong to no man, who may not have speedy remedy"; and a representative assembly elected by the freemen. In addition, laws passed by the company would be submitted to the General Assembly before going into effect, an important protection against an inept or insensitive administration in England. Such reforms, Purchas concluded, "hath caused the Colony now at length to settle themselves in a firme resolution to perpetuate the Plantation."

Reforms in the colony's economy kept pace with those in government. Like Captain John Smith, Sandys believed the colony's salvation to be in such basic products as silk, wine, and iron rather than in the ephemeral quest for gold and the South Sea, or for get-rich-quick crops of tobacco and sassafras. Smith must have noted with keen approval the company's efforts to diversify the economy, to which only he, and briefly

Lord de la Warr, had paid anything but lip service. Sandys insisted on salt for preserving fish (to be made principally, and appropriately, on Smith's Island outside Chesapeake Bay), cordage, timber, pitch, and tar as well as the commodities long expected from Virginia. Determined to do things right this time, the company did not stint in seeking experienced artisans for its projects. It sent to Virginia several "French Vignerons or Vine-men" to make wine, salters (including another Frenchman) to staff the saltworks, four "skilfull men from Germany" to set up sawmills, and several other men to work the iron mines under the supervision of John Berkeley, "a Gentleman of an Honourable Family." Between 1618 and 1622 the company spent almost £500 on iron production alone. And with an eye to profiting from the Indians, the Sandys administration earmarked £200 in goods for the fur trade, and sent glassblowers to make beads for barter.

Agriculture received attention too. The London Company sent scores of workers to the public lands, some to be under Captain Thomas Nuce on the company land, some under resident treasurer George Sandys (Sir Edwin's brother), some under William Nuce, the new marshall. Ships arriving at Jamestown brought other tenants for secretary Pory, for George Thorpe who directed the college lands, and for Doctor Lawrence Bohune, the colony physician, who also received "divers Appothecaries and Surgeons." Perhaps 3,500 immigrants — some sent by the company, some by private patentees — arrived in the first years of the Sandys-Southampton administration.

During the early 1620s Virginia's backers found still another sign of progress. The colony would soon have educational facilities. By 1622 two separate but interrelated projects had emerged: a grammar school and university for English youths, and a college for Indians. The school, to be erected at Charles City "as the most commodious place for health, security, profit, and conveniency," had its origin in 1621 at the Cape of Good Hope. There Chaplain Patrick Copland of the East

India Company's *Royal James* persuaded the captain and crew to contribute £70.8.6 for some charitable work in Virginia; Copland and the company decided that the colony most needed a free school. The company therefore assigned one thousand acres and several workers to the projected "East India School," named in honor of its first benefactors. The company also prepared to send someone to teach "the principles of Religion, civility of life, and humane learning"; it expected to have a university at Henrico City by the time the scholars were ready for more advanced studies.

The Indian college, stemming from the determination of Englishmen to "reduce the barbarous [Indians] to more civilitie" and convert them to Anglicanism, would be a separate and unique unit of the university. Like the other educational ventures it would depend on contributions from the mother country and proceeds from company lands. Samuel Purchas hailed it as "a Seminarie and Schoole of education to the Natives"; it would obviate the need to send Indan children to England "to be taught our language and letters" as had been done in small numbers for some years. It would also replace the scattered efforts of the Virginia clergy, three of whom had received £24 each from Nicholas Ferrar to raise several Indian youths "in Christian Religion, and some good course to live by." Ferrar's bequest provided an additional £300 for the college when it enrolled ten Indians. Plans moved ahead rapidly. While the company successfully recruited more donors, George Thorpe labored to make the college lands profitable, and the General Assembly sought Indian students. Each plantation, it decreed, must "obtaine unto themselves by just meanes" several native youths, "Of which children the most towardly boyes in witt & graces of nature [are] to be brought up by them in the firste Elements of litterature, so as to be fitted for the Colledge intended for them. . . ."

John Smith played no active role in Virginia colonization during the busy years of reform, but he read with interest the reports that lavishly praised the colony's achievements. Its recent settlers were choice men, the company boasted, "borne and bred up to labour and industry." They had built new, sturdy houses for themselves and guest houses for newcomers. They had planted vineyards and gardens, and had made encouraging progress in mining and manufacturing. Grateful for the improved state of the colony, the General Assembly in the fall of 1621 voted, with "alacritie and cheerefulnesse," its thanks to the London Company. After only a few years in office, propagandists of the Sandys-Southampton admininistration proclaimed (Smith would not have been so sure) Virginia "by the blessing of Almighty God is growne to good perfection."

Slave labor on a Virginia plantation

VIII

Toward an American Society

For almost a quarter-century John Smith watched Virginia grow. During some of that time he served British America directly; at other times he promoted settlement through his pen or through his influence with the architects of empire. He did not, of course, fully understand the potential of the New World, but along with a few other men of vision, Smith saw that America would be more than a mere copy or extension of England. What Smith sensed, and Americans later took for granted, was that England's institutions could not be transferred *in toto* to the American strand, Too much of her culture defied transplantation: the feudal vestiges, the entrenched nobility, the commercial and cultural vitality of London, the intellectual vigor of Oxford and Cambridge, the ebb and flow of people across the channel to centers of European civilization.

America lay three thousand miles away. British colonists would never be totally isolated, but as settlement moved inexorably inland, and as new generations emerged without experiential ties to the Old World, Virginia and the other British colonies increasingly reflected their American setting at the expense of their English origin. Patterns of representative government, ethnic diversity, religious pluralism, servile labor, intense population growth and innumerable other distinctive characteristics — some profound, some superficial — heralded a new society. Many of the trends began in John Smith's lifetime.

Not all of the first colony's examples were laudable. As Puritan leader John Winthrop observed on the eve of his departure for New England, Virginia's mistakes "hathe taught all other plantations to prevent the like occasions." It had, among other faults, "used unfitt instrumentes, a multitude of rude and misgovernd persons[,] the very scumme of the Land." That familiar charge had been made earlier by John Smith and his successors in the Virginia government, as well as by the company and its spokesmen in England. Yet the crux of the labor problem in the first decade, and occasionally thereafter, lay as much in the untimely arrival of the settlers as in their poor quality. Even good workers meant more mouths to feed and more houses to build; short rations and inadequate shelter assured heavy mortality and consequent problems of recruitment. Gradually the colony's ability to absorb newcomers improved and the demand for workers mounted.

In the long run, demand far exceeded supply. The tasks to be done in a frontier society knew no limits: clearing forests, planting crops, and constructing shelter required immense energy. The colony needed men to fell trees and saw them into timber and boards; it needed men to build houses, churches, wharves, and bridges; it needed men to sow corn, wheat, and peas, and still others to catch fish and hunt for game. And there was always the necessity of redoing much that had been done too hastily or too ineptly at first. Houses made of unseasoned wood had to be rebuilt. Indian attacks destroyed buildings and crops. Tobacco rapidly wore out the soil so new fields had to be cleared and roads laid to reach them. Virginia could easily have employed every surplus worker in Stuart England.

Sir Thomas Dale proposed one solution. If for three years the King would banish to the colony all men condemned to die, Virginia would be adequately furnished with workers

"and not allwayes with the worst kinde of men either for
birth, spiritts or Bodie, and sutch who wold be right glad so to
escape a just sentence to make this their new Countrie and
plant and inhabite therein with all diligence, cheerfullnes and
Comfort." A few criminals did, in fact, come to Virginia, but
never in significant numbers during the seventeenth century.
Yet Dale saw the principal need: colonists whose self-interest
would tie them to Virginia's future.

The solution to the labor problem lay in attracting able
men, not in emptying jails or criticizing incompetents. For a
while the company tried to screen the moral and professional
qualifications of applicants, with little success. More urgent
were incentives to lure good workers, either as independent
craftsmen or in temporary service to others. Most urgent were
spurs to permanency and stability. Long-term projects such as
silk and iron works had little chance of success if a majority of
the settlers intended to stay in Virginia only until they raised
a few lucrative crops of tobacco, or tried their hand at dis-
covering precious metals, or perhaps simply escaped for a
while an awkward situation at home. As John Rolfe observed:
"the vulgar sort looked for supplies out of England [and]
neglected husbandry." A sound economy, a stable government,
and a congenial populace could not be realized until most of
the colonists thought of America as a permanent home.

The London Company belatedly recognized that no all-
male community could be permanent. No women came in the
first expedition because of the expected hardships, but passengers on the second supply included a Mistress Forrest, wife
of Thomas Forrest, gentleman, and her maid Ann Burras. As
the only single woman in a colony of lusty Englishmen, Miss
Burras could hardly have remained unattached for long. She
soon married John Laydon, a laborer who had sailed with the
first voyage. Subsequent ships brought more women and some
children, so that family life gradually became part of the
colonial scene. Yet the bulk of the early settlers continued to
be single men; their cultural prejudices precluded marriage to

Indians, and unmarried Englishwomen seldom journeyed to America.

Eventually the company decided to recruit and ship prospective brides. On 3 November 1619, Sir Edwin Sandys proposed to send one hundred "Maides young and uncorrupt" to Virginia "to make the men there more setled & lesse moveable who by defect thereof (as is credibly reported) stay there but to gett something and then to returne for England, which will breed a dissolucion, and so an overthrow of the Plantacion." Sandys urged the company to bear the transportation costs of women who married tenants of the company; the rest were to be paid for by "those that takes them to wife." Sometime in late 1619 or early 1620 the company sent ninety young women to Virginia, and in July of the latter year promised to provide one hundred more. In 1621 the company established a separate joint stock, with subscriptions totalling £800, for additional "younge handsome and honestly educated maydes," so that "the Planters mindes may be the faster tyed to Virginia by the bondes of Wyves and Children." Impoverished youths were also shipped to Virginia. In 1618 the city of London dispatched "an hundred younge boyes and girles that lay starving in the streetes." Sandys encouraged this and subsequent contingents, for in Virginia they would work as apprentices and "under severe Masters . . . be brought to goodnes." Although aimed as much at lessening the population of England as at increasing the labor supply of Virginia, the transportation of children had important implications for domestic life as well: girls would serve until marriage (or age twenty-one if not married sooner), and thus add to the number of eligible brides.

Little is known about the women who volunteered to be wives in America. As early as 1618 (a year before any were sent), John Chamberlain heard a rumor that a London rogue had been recruiting "rich yeomens daughters . . . to serve his Majestie for breeders in Virginia." Several years later a critic of the Smythe regime charged that Sir Thomas had sent "but few women thither & those corrupt." The Sandys-Southampton administration claimed that its prospective brides had good morals. They were to have good care too, with proper food and housing on arrival, and those not quickly wedded must board in households already containing a married woman. Whatever the women's backgrounds and morals, their hopes and disappointments, they were welcomed, literally with open arms. Samuel Purchas reported that 57 maids went to Virginia in 1621, "divers of which were well married before the comming away of the Ships." And as with any scarce commodity, prices rapidly climbed out of reach of all but the wealthy. "Women are necessary members of the Colonye," one disgruntled male wrote in 1623, "but the poore men are never the nearer for them they are so well sould. . . ." The company as well as the marketplace had a hand in that situation: in 1621 it set the price of a wife at 120 pounds of best leaf tobacco, soon raised to 150 pounds. It also directed the governor to see that no woman married a servant unless she "unwarily or fondly bestow her self" upon him; far better, the governor was advised, to steer the maids "to such freemen or tennetes as have meanes to manteine them." To those who married the brides it sent, the company promised to consign the first available servants — a lure intended to attract additional marriageable women. That lure did not work as well as the company hoped. For many years a severe shortage of women continued, enabling a few to indulge in bigamy "to the great contempt of the Majestie of God and ill example to others."

Throughout the seventeenth century a disparity of sexes kept Virginia's population growth below that of other British colonies. But after 1619 Virginia was more than a temporary refuge for English males; family life became the norm. Even with a relatively high ratio of men to women among newcomers, Virginia's population expanded rapidly in response to large families, low mortality, and heavy immigration. From about 350 whites in 1616 the colony grew to nearly 15,000 by mid-century and to over 60,000 by 1700. By that time the number of whites in all of British America had reached a quarter million.

As the colony grew, its people became more ethnically diverse. Although few in absolute numbers, Frenchmen, Germans, Swiss, Italians, Poles, and at least one Armenian gave early Virginia a somewhat international flavor. Throughout the century immigration from continental Europe remained sparse, but a precedent had been established. In the eighteenth century Virginia, and especially neighboring Pennsylvania, attracted large contingents of non-English whites. Some remained in ethnic enclaves, but many intermarried with other nationalities to create a hybrid American stock. Except in rare instances, however, Americans of European descent did not mix with the Indian or African races; rather, swelling numbers of Africans became separated by law and custom from white society while the neighboring Indians, sharply reduced by disease and war, moved west in the face of white expansion. Ethnic diversity, but not racial fusion, marked England's colonies.

Early Virginia also acquired diversity in religion, despite repeated attempts to keep the colony strictly Anglican. As early as 1609, Robert Johnson, an alderman of London and a leading figure in the company, insisted that Virginia accept only immigrants who would "keepe conformitie with the lawes, language and religion of England for ever." That meant no papists and no Puritans. To most Englishmen of Johnson's day Roman Catholicism smacked of treason; Spain was their symbol of Catholic power and Guy Fawkes of an Englishman who had succumbed to "the scarlet whore." Robert Gray, writing in the same year as Alderman Johnson, urged the ministers to resist popery, "for as it doth infect the mind with errour, so it doth infect the manners of men with disloyaltie and treachery. . . ." Crown, company, and colony all issued proscriptions against settlement by Catholics. Very few came to Virginia in the seventeenth century.

Puritanism proved harder to exclude. Because it arose as a movement within the Church of England, no sharp distinctions set its members off from the more orthodox. As the strength of the faction grew in England during Virginia's first twenty-five years, ripples from the groundswell reached the distant colony. Reverend Robert Hunt, chosen for the first expedition to Virginia by Richard Hakluyt with the approval of the Archbishop of Canterbury, was orthodox enough. In 1609, however, Reverend William Mease brought dissenting views and religious discord, "being, as they say, somewhat a puritane," with the result that "the most part refused to go to his service, or to heare his sermons, though by the other part he was supported & favored. . . ." Mease stayed on until 1620, apparently without altering the thrust of his preaching. In 1611 he gained a spiritual colleague in Alexander Whitaker, son of a celebrated Cambridge University professor. Whitaker had barely set foot in British America before he appealed to Reverend William Crashaw of London for "any young Godly and learned Ministers whom the Church of England hath not, or refuseth, to sett a worke." "We have noe need either of ceremonies or bad livers. Discretion and learninge, zeal with knowledge would doe much good." In the language of Jacobean England, that was a call for Puritan preachers. But the request fell on deaf ears. "I much more muse," Reverend Whitaker noted a few years later, "that so few of our English Ministers that were so hot against the Surplis and subscription: come thither, where neither [are] spoken of." The clergymen who came to Virginia during John Smith's lifetime adhered to more orthodox practices. In 1619 the General Assembly decided that "All ministers shall duely read divine service, and exercise their ministerial function according to the Ecclesiasticall Lawes and orders of the churche of *Englande*," a rule which left little room for Puritan ministers and which may explain the departure in 1620 of William Mease. Whitaker had drowned in 1617.

Thanks, then, to the energy of the London Company and

the resident assembly on the one hand, and to the paucity of
Puritan clergymen on the other, Virginia emerged by 1630 as a
bastion of religious conformity. It did not remain one. In the
1630s Puritan infiltration resumed and by 1648 had so upset
the Anglican majority that the General Assembly ordered the
expulsion of all nonconformists. Although most of the Puritans
moved to Maryland or Massachusetts, and although the
Church of England remained Virginia's only legally established faith, other denominations made inroads. By the end of
the century small groups of Presbyterians, Baptists, and
Quakers worshipped freely. The trend toward diversity and
grudging toleration, paralleled by events in the other English
colonies, continued and broadened in the eighteenth century.

Virginia's ecclesiastical structure, like its theological pro-
pensity, began by reflecting England's — at least on the surface. Underneath Virginia differed significantly from the
mother country, for the absence of a hierarchy caused the
established church to evolve in a uniquely American fashion.
Without bishops and their superiors there could be no ecclesiastical courts, no close inspection of priests, not even ordina-
tion ceremonies. Hence individual parishes enjoyed a large
measure of autonomy, usually exercised through the local
vestrymen who arrogated the right to select their pastors and
to supervise all parish matters. In the long run, the structure
of the church in Virginia would resemble the Puritan churches
of New England where local autonomy was explicit. By the
time the Puritans established their independent congrega-
tions, Virginians had long enjoyed a similar polity but with
considerably less fanfare. If the later areas of English colonization in America did not consciously follow Virginia's example,
they at least conformed to a pattern she had known from the
outset.

The availability of land played a major part in the growth
of a large and contented white population. In England land
meant more than material possession; it brought its owner

prestige and social distinction. It also carried the key to political participation because of the property qualification for voting — a requirement few in England could meet. Land ownership therefore had an irresistible attraction to Englishmen of John Smith's time.

The first settlers in Virginia received no land. They shared in later distributions, of course, but they wanted quicker wealth. When that dream faded they rapidly lost their willingness, lukewarm from the outset, to work communally on company land and be provisioned from the company store. In 1614 Sir Thomas Dale ameliorated the situation by allotting three acres of garden land to each man. The results were dramatic. "When our people were fedde out of the common store and laboured jointly," Ralph Hamor related, ". . . glad was that man that could slippe from his labour, nay the most honest of them in a generall businesse, would not take so much faithfull and true paines, in a weeke, as now he will doe in a day. . . ." By the "blessing of God, and their owne industry," Hamor insisted, all now prospered. Still, the company retained title to the land; not until 1617 did it begin to assign freeholds. Old planters received one hundred acres and the promise of as much in a second division, while the headright system encouraged the distribution of still more land. Virginians of little wealth soon learned "the sweetnesse of proprietie." At the same time, many a penniless Englishman contracted to work in America for a number of years, usually seven in the early period but four or five by mid-century, in the hope that at the end of his servitude he too could acquire land. And usually he could. In Virginia and other colonies the "freedom dues" granted to a servant on expiration of his indenture often included land as well as clothing, livestock, and weapons; if not, cheap land was easy to find.

Skilled craftsmen, as well as common laborers, felt the pull. England had a surplus of most kinds of artisans; in the early years of the seventeenth century they could stay home and starve or migrate to Ireland or Spain or even North Africa.

Virginia seemed a preferable alternative and the London Company tried hard to lure them. Frequent broadsides and promotional pamphlets advertised the colony's wants. In 1610 the company sought the esoteric crafts of pearl drillers, silk dressers, and preservers of caviar, as well as the usual blacksmiths, sawyers, coopers, and rope makers. With ill health a continuing problem, there were repeated calls for surgeons and apothecaries. By 1620 the catalogue of most wanted occupations had changed significantly: experts in pearls and caviar no longer made the list, giving way to more practical craftsmen — weavers, tanners, fishhook makers, lime burners.

For artisans the lure of Virginia lay as much in high wages as in the availability of work and land. "Yea I say," a settler wrote to John Smyth of Nibley in 1622, "that any laborious honest man may in a shorte time become ritche in this Country." Although government-imposed ceilings curtailed colonial wages until the mid-1620s, they substantially exceeded those in England. The colonial carpenter, bricklayer, or cooper earned four shillings per day (three if the employer provided meat and drink); in London the same craftsman received about half as much. In America one had to work hard of course. John Smith made clear in his *Description of New England* that loafers would not find the New World easy, but for men with energy the rewards were bountiful: "here every man may be master and owner of his owne labour and land; or the greatest part in a small time. If hee have nothing but his hands, he may set up his trade; and by industrie quickly grow rich. . . ."

With high wages and abundant real estate, Virginia gradually acquired the aura of a promised land. Especially under the Sandys-Southampton administration, thousands of Englishmen braved the long Atlantic crossing to share its opportunities. Only the frightful mortality of Virginia's first two decades kept the colony from quickly gaining a population of several thousand artisans and laborers whom England did not want and for whom British America became both haven and home.

Not that poor men became rich overnight. The need to clear land and to import tools and other manufactured goods, and the frequent setbacks from crop failures and Indian attacks, prevented many from realizing the handsome profits they had been led to expect. English propagandists insisted that "they which goe away from hence very poore may within a little while become very rich: they that here were but needy & of mean estate, may there arise to be, as we terme men of substance and good abilitie." That statement came from a man who never set foot in America. Yet hundreds and eventually tens of thousands of Englishmen shared implicitly the sentiments of a Plymouth colonist, quoted in 1621 by John Smith. "We are all freeholders," the Pilgrim wrote; "the rent day doth not trouble us. . . ." That was incentive enough for most immigrants.

A few men did acquire large estates and handsome profits. George Yeardley, Ralph Hamor, and others took advantage of their shares in the company, their membership in the council of state, and the headright system to accumulate sizable holdings. By engrossing the available supply of workers they assured themselves of substantial tobacco profits and hence the opportunity to buy the next batch of servants. ("Our principall wealth," noted Virginia's secretary of state John Pory in 1619, ". . . consisteth in servants.") The ownership of servants led, in turn, to the acquisition of still more land, either for immediate use or for speculation. And with extensive landholdings went political influence. The few men of aristocratic birth who came to Virginia enjoyed considerable power regardless of their holdings; as John Rolfe observed, to become "a firme and perfect Common-weale," the colony needed men "of birth and quallyty to command." However, most men who rose to prominence launched their careers from a solid platform of real estate. To protect their investments in land

and labor and to fulfill their obligation to the community, they took on the chores of local and colony-wide government. They also acquired, as far as they could, the appurtenances of a social elite. The seeds of a plantation aristocracy, which would mature in the next century, were sown in John Smith's lifetime.

Virginians assumed that the socially prominent were entitled to special privileges. Even during Smith's brief stay, the colony deferred to the "better sorte" — a category that barely included the captain, whose reluctance to cater to the whims of his social superiors earned their enmity. "In *Virginia*," he later wrote (and probably said aloud while there), "a plaine Souldier that can use a pick-axe and spade, is better than five Knights. . . ." He even forced gentlemen colonists to swing an ax — a rare and unpleasant experience for them — and added insult to injury by pouring a can of water down an offender's sleeve for each oath his blistered hands provoked. Smith, as a proto-American, was ahead of his time. More typical was George Percy who in 1611 complained that he was falling in debt, "it standing upon my reputation (being Governor of James Towne) to keep a continuall and dayly Table for Gentlemen of fashion about me. . . ." Most colonists clung incorrigibly to such inherited concepts of class privilege. Wrote William Strachey: "I have heard the inferioor people, with alacrity of spirit professe, that they should never refuse to doe their best . . . when such worthy, and Noble Gentlemen goe in and out before them." Occasionally someone challenged the elite's prerogatives, but to little avail. In 1624 a settler charged that "neither the Governor nor the Counsell could or would doe any poore men right, but . . . would shew favor to great men and wronge the poore." He was close to the mark. That same year the Assembly ruled that bigamy be punished "according to the qualitie of the person so offending."

With social distinction went as much pomp as the poor colony could muster. William Strachey described for English readers the deference accorded its governor as early as 1610:

"Every Sunday, when the Lord Governour, and Captain Generall goeth to Church, hee is accompanied with all the Counsailers, Captaines, other Officers, and all the Gentlemen, and with a Guard of Holberdiers in his Lordship's Livery, faire red cloakes, to the number of fifty, both on each side, and behinde him: and being in the Church, his Lordship hath his seate in the Quier, in a greene Velvet Chaire, with a Cloath, with a Velvet Cushion spread on a Table before him, on which he kneeleth; . . . and when he returneth home againe, he is waited on to his house in the same manner." Virginia might be a frontier community, but it could not quite forget its English manners.

In many respects, then, the colony imitated the social structure of the mother country. But distinctly non-English characteristics appeared too. Virginia had proportionately fewer men without land of their own, fewer men of inherited prestige, and almost no representatives of the upper reaches of England's social hierarchy. (Lord de la Warr was the only peer to serve in Virginia until the 1680s.) More than a century later, Hector St. John de Crevecoeur would assert that America had "no aristocratic families, no courts, no kings, no bishops. . . . The rich and the poor are not so far removed from each other as they are in Europe." That pattern had begun to emerge in John Smith's day; by the time he laid down his pen in 1631, middle-class upstarts rather than gentlemen of distinguished families dominated Virginia society.

The colony's lack of material refinements helps to explain its paucity of English gentlemen. Wilderness life offered few of the traditional symbols of social status. A gentleman might long for a larger and more ornate house than his neighbors, but the wattle and daub buildings of the early years only gradually gave way to timber and brick; the carpenter-architects of 1630 had not yet found time for manor houses. A gentleman might also crave a horse and carriage, but they would be of little use in a land without roads. Some luxury had begun to appear through the importation of British finery bought with profits from tobacco; wine too could be imported. (Despite the best efforts of the company, the colony failed to produce good and abundant wine.) But here again the customs of England began to give way to customs uniquely American. Englishmen raised on wine and beer discovered that in the colonies they had to drink water or find some other potion. In 1620 George Thorpe announced an acceptable substitute. "Wee have found a waie," he wrote to John Smyth of Nibley, "to make soe good drinke of Indian corne as I protest I have divers times refused to drinke stronge Englishe beare and chosen to drinke that." Corn liquor soon became a Virginia staple.

If the New World lacked some of the luxury of the Old, it offered adequate compensation to people of modest needs. Writing to Sir Dudley Carleton in 1619, John Pory confessed that "at my first coming hither the solitary uncouthnes of this place, compared to those partes of Christendome or Turky where I had bene . . . did not a little vexe me." But, he added, Virginia had many attractions. The flora and fauna were equal or superior to England's, tobacco promised rapid wealth for the industrious, and the governor had so benefitted from his position that he became rich in a few years. And even the lowly enjoyed some elegance. "We are not the veriest beggers in the worlde," Pory boasted, "our cowekeeper here of James citty on Sundays goes accowtered all in freshe flaming silke; and a wife of one that in England had professed the black arte, not of a scholler, but of a collier of Croyden, weares her rough bever hatt with a faire perle hatband, and a silken suite thereto correspondent." With allowance for exaggeration, Pory had accurately characterized British America. A colony had emerged where common people could realize in a few years a material prosperity out of reach at home.

America's social and economic opportunity had an invidious underside. Two increasingly significant groups enjoyed neither prestige nor property: white indentured servants and African forced labor. Most of the former, however, could look forward to eventual freedom and land ownership. In the meantime they endured the unenviable status of bondsmen, which often — for both blacks and whites — meant barely humane treatment. But the need to attract English laborers mitigated the maltreatment of indentured whites; they could hardly be expected to flock to Virginia if, like Thomas Best, they were treated "like a damnd slave." Black servants, on the other hand, had not come willingly nor could they warn away their countrymen in Africa. The status of blacks became increasingly debased. Virginia's social structure thus acquired a range as great as England's but significantly different; it began and ended lower on the scale than the mother country's. By 1630, or soon after, the colony claimed nothing closer to royalty or high nobility than a governor of modest social credentials and a handful of nouveau-riche landlords, while the bottom point of American society rested on permanent and inheritable bondage — something England had long since abandoned.

The first blacks came to Virginia in 1619, a decade after John Smith's departure. He and other Englishmen learned of their arrival through a letter written in late 1619 or early 1620 "By me John Rolfe" and published in Smith's *Generall Historie*. The previous summer, Rolfe noted, "our governour and councell caused Burgesses to be chosen in all places, and met at a generall Assembly, where all matters were debated [which were] thought expedient for the good of the Colony. . . ." The next paragraph laconically recorded that "About the last of August came in a dutch man of warre that sold us twenty Negars. . . ." Neither John Smith nor anyone else at the time found ironic the almost simultaneous emergence of representative government and Negro bondage. Seventeenth-century Englishmen on both sides of the Atlantic failed to recognize that the former institution would soon evolve into a bulwark of liberty for white men, the latter into an agency of total servility for blacks.

Because of the overwhelming implications of the introduction of black labor into Virginia, historians have long debated the status of the first Africans to enter the mainland colonies and the shadowy process by which their descendants and other black immigrants became victims of a system of bondage not practiced elsewhere in the British Empire. The problem results mainly from a shortage of evidence: records were not kept, or did not survive, to document the emergence of permanent and inheritable servitude as the predominant condition for blacks in colonial America. Partly, though, the historical problem stems from semantics: "slave" and "servant" have fairly precise definitions in the twentieth century; in the seventeenth they had vague and inconsistent meanings. Early American slavery has therefore been shrouded in confusion as well as obscurity, open to a variety of plausible but conflicting interpretations.

But much of the story is clear. Seventeenth-century Englishmen inherited from Elizabethan culture several preconceptions of profound importance for the emergence of Negro slavery. First, they harbored a deeply imbedded revulsion toward *blackness,* which the English mind readily projected onto the dark-skinned people of Africa. Second, Englishmen possessed, or were possessed by, an ethnocentric view of cultural differences. The English way was correct and superior; the further another society deviated from the English model, the greater its error and inferiority. Finally, although England no longer practiced slavery or serfdom in the sense of inheritable lifetime bondage, it recognized a wide range of unfree statuses that permitted ownership of another's labor, and even to some extent his person.

The Englishman's antipathy to blackness is easier to describe than to explain. Elizabethans had long associated the color black with dirt, evil, sin, and death. It was, in short, "an emotionally partisan color." The danger of that partisanship bore bitter fruit in the late sixteenth century when Englishmen experienced their first contact with West Africa. Immediately and unconsciously they transferred to the dark-skinned inhabitants the very qualities they had already associated with blackness. Thus the Englishman who came to Virginia in the early seventeenth century brought an assumption — subconscious perhaps and seldom articulated — that a man with a black skin must be intrinsically unclean, dangerous, and inferior; he was "blacke and lothsome." In the revealing words of Captain John Smith, Africans came from "those fryed Regions of blacke brutish Negers."

Ethnocentricity reinforced color prejudice. Englishmen, like all other peoples, preferred their own customs, language, and beliefs. But because of England's relative isolation from other ethnic groups, and because of her relatively homogeneous population, her citizens carried their self-appreciation to unusual heights, looking with suspicion and distrust on most of their non-English contemporaries, even the neighboring Scots and especially the Irish. Irishmen appeared uncouth and unruly. Africans, with unfamiliar physical features and with strikingly non-English habits of clothing, of housing, of daily life, not to mention their language, political systems, and economy, seemed absolutely barbarous. Especially appalling to Englishmen was African religion, for at the core of their cultural myopia lay an uncompromising conviction that their own brand of theology, and no other, had divine sanction. If they did not actually say "God is an Englishman," John Smith and his contemporaries acted on that assumption. Hence an African who held to his native ways was triply damned: by his skin, by his customs, and by his faith.

Englishmen might have avoided all association with Africans, and to a large extent they did. Contacts between England and Africa were few and far between; even the slave trade of the seventeenth and eighteenth centuries involved only a few hundred English sailors and a handful of resident agents who directed their deplorable commerce at the New World rather than the Old. England did not need black labor.

America did. In Virginia, a shortage of able-bodied workers lasted the lifespan of British America. Tobacco called insatiably for cheap labor, a call that thousands answered; but disease killed an alarming portion of the Europeans who came during the early years. For the survivors, inexpensive land offered a chance to become employers, with a consequent increase in the demand for workers. Gradually, Africans provided the solution. Only a few arrived in the first decades; at mid-century the colony contained about 300. By 1681, however, the figure had increased ten-fold and in 1708 it had jumped to 12,000 out of a total population of 60,000. By that time African labor, both imported and American-born, formed the keystone of the colony's economy. In the mid-eighteenth century blacks comprised forty to fifty per cent of Virginia's population and were a sizable majority in many counties. And the other English colonies had exploited African labor too, though most of them on a lesser scale. In 1760 twenty per cent of all British Americans were black, almost all of them enslaved.

Africans brought to Virginia could, in theory, have served under indentures much like white laborers, and a few during the early decades probably did. But several factors made that option unlikely in the long run. First, England permitted various forms of servitude in which apprentices, paupers, vagrants, debtors, criminals, prisoners of war and others could be forced to labor for long periods, even for life. The status of blacks, seized in Africa as booty and sold as captives, closely paralleled that of war prisoners; they thus brought with them a stigma that permitted life servitude without violating England's legal or social guidelines. The potential for a system of total bondage made the transit to America as part of the Virginian's cultural baggage.

The precedents of the New World were as impelling as the

prejudices of the Old. By 1619, when the first blacks arrived in Virginia, more than a quarter-million had already been brought to the Americas, principally to the Spanish and Portuguese possessions in South America and the West Indies, and a few to the English island of Bermuda. (Little is known of Bermuda's first blacks; presumably they were treated like Virginia's.) Aware from the publications of Hakluyt and Purchas, and later of John Smith, that the Spanish subjected Africans to permanent and inheritable bondage, Virginians must have considered enslavement the most obvious and logical option, especially since many blacks arrived after being "seasoned" to slavery in the West Indies. In the absence of moral or legal qualms, and in the presence of deep-seated racial and cultural biases and a persistent labor shortage, it is hard to imagine slavery *not* taking root in British America.

The pre-1619 attitudes of Virginians toward Africans can only be argued abstractly; the crucial test of early black-white relations lies in what Anglo-Virginians did with African immigrants after 1619. Again, the records are frustratingly scarce, but enough have survived to permit a few reliable generalizations: (1) some blacks gained freedom and became landowners and perhaps voters; (2) Virginians from the outset treated blacks as a different and inferior people; (3) slavery rapidly developed as the black man's lot, some probably suffering that status by the time of John Smith's death in 1631, most of them by the 1640s.

That at least a few blacks became free during the early decades of Afro-American history is incontrovertible, though how they acquired freedom is not. Some may have served for a term of years and then been emancipated by masters who assumed that blacks were entitled to liberty after as many or perhaps a few more years than white servants. Most or all of the Christianized blacks probably escaped permanent bondage, for a corollary to the Englishman's assumption of heathenism's inferiority held that no Christian should keep another in bondage. (Theological opinion remained divided on that point.) Other black servants may have been manumitted by humane owners; still others may have bought their own freedom with wages their masters allowed them to earn. In 1625, for example, a Negro named Brass received forty pounds of tobacco per month for serving Lady Yeardley; at that time he was either free or being accorded unusually liberal privileges for a servant in early Virginia. Of those early blacks who are known to have gained freedom, several acquired property and even modest amounts of wealth and distinction. At least one black man, Anthony Johnson, received headright allotments for paying the transportation to Virginia of several other persons, and he owned one or more slaves.

In spite of the occasional examples of free and even prosperous Negroes in early seventeenth-century Virginia, the evidence of widespread and virulent prejudice against blacks in general is even more impressive. In 1627, eight years after the arrival of the first Africans, Governor George Yeardley's will left to his heirs "goode debts, chattles, servants, negars, cattle or any other thing." The "negars" may have been servants too, but a separate listing for them suggests at least that blacks were considered apart, presumably inferior, and certainly as a species of property; at most the sequence of Yeardley's listing in which Negroes come between servants and cattle suggests lifetime servitude, a crucial ingredient of full-fledged slavery.

Other records confirm the implications of Yeardley's will. In 1630 the Virginia Court sentenced Hugh Davis, a white man convicted of fornicating with a black woman, to be flogged "before an assembly of negroes and others for abusing himself to the dishonor of God and shame of Christians, by defiling his body in lying with a negro," an indication of the greater sin imputed to interracial sex and thus of the demeaned status of blacks. In 1639 the Assembly prohibited Negroes from bearing arms, another sign that they were feared and distrusted and treated as a separate category. By the 1640s black women, but not white, were expected to do field work and to be counted as tithables, a discrimination in taxation that paralleled the barring of black men from the militia. And consistently, Virginia censuses of the early years listed blacks uniquely and usually anonymously: lists of inhabitants in the 1620s identified white servants by name and often by age, ship, and date of arrival; blacks usually by the number of them at a given locality—no name, no age, no additional data. In the few instances in which blacks are listed by name, the census customarily gave a first name only, followed by "Negro" or its Dutch or Spanish equivalent.

That slavery developed soon after 1619 is clear from a variety of scattered evidence. Perhaps the "negars" in Governor Yeardley's will or the blacks recorded elsewhere were serving for terms of years; perhaps too the absence of dates of arrival in the early censuses — documenting the starting point of an indenture — did not preclude eventual release from servitude. But as early as 1639, neighboring Maryland guaranteed the rights of Englishmen to "all Inhabitants of this Province being Christians (Slaves excepted)," and, in a similar vein, set the term for Christian servants arriving without a written indenture at four years, "Slaves excepted." By the 1640s other signs suggest permanent bondage for a substantial portion of Virginia's blacks: the higher prices paid for black servants, the higher values assigned to blacks in their owner's inventories and wills, and the failure of such lists to specify the number of years remaining to be served by black servants corroborate an observation of 1652 that it "is a common course practiced amongst English men to buy negers, to that end they may have them for service or slaves forever. . . ." While statutory recognition of perpetual and inheritable servitude for most Negroes did not come until 1661, its practice had clearly begun earlier, for law followed custom as surely in early Virginia as anywhere else. The paucity of blacks during the early decades made legislation unnecessary, and the absence of specific precedents in English law may have made legislators wary. But by the 1660s slavery had become sufficiently widespread and entrenched to command the attention of the colony's legislators who then fashioned legal underpinnings for an institution already beginning to thrive. By the third quarter of the century, *slave,* a term seldom used in England or the colonies prior to this time except to indicate war captives or other totally subjected individuals, had found its modern usage.

The failure of Rolfe or John Smith to comment on the role of the first Negroes in Virginia and on the insidious initial steps toward racial slavery reflected their era's relative indifference to social issues. Smith and his countrymen cared more for imperial, commercial, and religious matters; blacks were too few and too unimportant in Virginia to command Smith's attention. He had roamed the world, seen men of all kinds, and even acquired a modest toleration for people of other lands and other cultures. But his toleration was based largely on strength. Smith respected men he thought had power and influence. He was not concerned with the fate of Virginia's blacks, who seemed to him uncivilized heathens, somewhat less worthy because of their color and their lack of weapons than the Indians he had known at Jamestown. He may, however, have suspected that Africans would eventually meet Virginia's chronic labor needs. In 1630 he observed that Spaniards in the West Indies "are glad to buy *Negroes* in *Affrica* . . . which although they bee as idle and as devilish people as any in the world, yet they cause them quickly to bee their best servants." In the margin Smith added, "Note well."

For a while Smith had hoped that the Indians would be amenable to labor. So had Robert Gray whose *Good Speed to Virginia* of 1609 advocated using Indians but keeping them unskilled: "Our English tradesmen and Artificers are to be advised that they be warie in taking the Savages to bee aprentices to teach them their trade, seeing there be meanes of imployment sufficient besides to set many thousands on worke; and therefore not necessarie as yet to instruct them in our trades and mysteries." Too few Indians enjoyed performing menial chores in the white settlements to make the slightest dent on the labor problem. Besides, fear of the Indians, not only as individuals but as potential links to wholesale tribal assaults, precluded their extensive use as workers. The first General Assembly warned that Indians should be employed only in heavily settled areas, no more than five or six to a place, and that "good guard in the night be kept upon them, for generally (though some amongst many may proove good) they are trecherous people, & quickly gone when they have done a villany."

Thus only one race could meet America's labor needs: white workers were too scarce; red workers created as many problems as they solved; but black workers could be exploited with impunity. The first decades of English colonization, accordingly, saw American patterns of race relations take lasting shape: land and liberty for Europeans, distrust and exclusion for Indians, debasement and enslavement for Africans. During Britain's century and a half of colonial rule, a few Indians and a few blacks would gain substantial acceptance into the white society, but only on terms of complete subservience to the dominant culture. British America would end, as it had begun, deeply rent by racial inequity.

A European artist's version of the massacre of 1622

IX

Collapse of an Experiment

ON THURSDAY, 18 April 1622, Reverend Patrick Copland of Bow Church, Cheapside, intoned before the members of the London Company "A Sermon of Thanksgiving for the Happie Successe of the affayres in Virginia this last yeare." Copland's optimism soared: the difficulties of passage by sea had been eliminated, new crops and industries now flourished, and the abnormal mortality rate had finally declined. Gone were the dangers of famine and wretched lodging that had so often wracked those who survived the hazards of the sea. Gone too was the danger of Indian attack, for among "the *Wonderful workes* of the Lord" could be counted "a happie league of Peace and Amitie fondly concluded and faithfully kept, betweene the *English* and the *Natives,* that the feare of killing each other is now vanished away."

Copland erred on every point. Unknown to him or to anyone else in England, the seven years of peace between the English and Indian inhabitants of Virginia had ended abruptly four weeks earlier. Open and bitter hostility now marked the colony's race relations, and with renewed warfare came a return of the other hardships that had briefly been allayed.

After 1615, red and white Virginians had enjoyed a period of mutual understanding and even friendship — or so most Englishmen thought. The scattered settlements no longer feared the natives. Disagreements were rare, and most households welcomed neighboring Indians who "commonly lodged in their bed-chambers." According to Samuel Purchas, Opechancanough, Powhatan's heir, had only recently vowed that "the Skie should sooner fall" than the treaty between the English and Indians should end. But unknown to Purchas and other observers of the American experiment, Opechancanough had been harboring long suppressed grievances which burst to the surface in a sudden, brutal massacre. In its train came extreme suffering from the sea, from famine, and from inadequate shelter, as if to mock Reverend Copland's pious boasting.

The frenzied assault in the spring of 1622 shocked the colony and its supporters. The animosity of the early years, they assumed, had long since ended; it had reflected temporary misunderstandings, or Powhatan's deviousness, or the irresponsible acts of a few malicious settlers. And while both natives and colonists had suffered heavily in the battles of subsequent years, the Rolfe-Pocahontas marriage, the death of Powhatan, and tighter restrictions on the colonists had, presumably, put an end to racial warfare. Henceforth Indians and Englishmen would live in harmony.

The record of Indian-white relations since 1607 did not support such confidence. The natives had been anxious to acquire European goods, especially iron tools, and Powhatan had hoped for aid against his enemies. From the outset, however, the prospect of permanent English settlements alarmed the Indians. As early as August 1607, Sir Walter Cope could report to Lord Salisbury, on the basis of information brought home by Captain Newport, that the Indians "used our men well untill they found they begann to plant & fortefye. . . ." George Percy concurred. "The Savages murmured at our planting in the Countrie," he recalled, but he took consolation in a petty chief's assurance that all would be well if the English did the Indians no harm and took only "a little waste ground, which doth [neither] you nor any of us any good." That situation didn't last long. A Dutch chronicler noted that within two years of the founding of Jamestown, "the Indians, seeing that the English were beginning to multiply, were determined to starve them and drive them out."

While John Smith remained in Virginia, Powhatan's efforts to dislodge the colony were sporadic and half-hearted at best. Not that the chief misread English intentions. Smith himself recorded a revealing conversation of early 1609: "Captaine *Smith,* (saith the king) some doubt I have of your comming hither . . . for many do informe me, your comming is not for trade, but to invade my people and possesse my Country." Powhatan wanted peace. "Having seene the death of all my people thrice . . . I know the difference of peace and warre better then any in my Countrie." If he fought the English, Powhatan predicted, he would "be so hunted by you that I can neither rest eat nor sleepe, but my tired men must watch, and if a twig but breake, everie one crie, there comes Captaine *Smith:* then must I flie I knowe not whether, and thus with miserable fear end my miserable life. . . ." Reluctantly the chief accepted the English presence.

By biding his time, Powhatan nearly won. Soon after Smith left Virginia the colony collapsed; in the spring of 1610 the Indians must have watched with satisfaction the evacuation of Jamestown, caused in no small part by their depredations. Then came de la Warr's relief expedition, the resettlement of Jamestown, and an English counteroffensive under Gates, Percy, and Dale. The Indians suffered devastating losses. After Argall seized Pocahontas as a hostage, they succumbed to treaties that called for almost total submission to the English. The bitterness of those early years lingered long after the principal actors had left the stage.

Beneath Indian resentment and English confidence lurked a more basic issue than land or force of arms: the contempt Englishmen felt for people they considered culturally inferior and religiously damned. Color was not an issue. The Indians, John Smith attested, were "of a colour browne when they are of any age, but they are borne white." Their skin darkened, Englishmen believed, from using skin dyes and ointments, or, according to John Rolfe, from living in smoky houses. On the whole the colonists admired Indian appearance.

They did not admire Indian theology. Conversion of the natives had been one of the initial aims of colonization, and although the early settlers made little progress in that direction the goal remained. So did the misconceptions on which it was based. Assuming that the Indians *wanted* to be converted (they "groane under the burden of the bondage of Satan," Patrick Copland maintained), and that for their own good the Indians *had* to be saved, authorities in England urged increasingly forceful tactics. First the settlers were admonished to woo the Indians to Christ by kindness and good example. When that failed, the company ordered more drastic measures: taking Indian children into English homes, subduing their chiefs, and imprisoning their priests. That hadn't worked either. By 1621 at least one Virginia clergyman saw no hope of converting the Indians "till their Priests and Ancients have their throats cut."

Acceptance of Christianity was only half the goal. The other half required the Indians to adopt the Englishman's version of "civilitie"; they must not remain "a rude, barbarous and naked people." In a sermon of 1622 to the London Company, the newly installed Dean of St. Paul's, John Donne, strongly advocated conversion of the Indians, but he insisted too that the colonists "Bring them to *love* and *Reverence* the name of that *King,* that sends men to teach them the wayes of *Civilitie* in this world," a sentiment John Smith reiterated two years later when he reminded his readers that adding colonists enlarged the King of England's honor "but the reducing Heathen people to civilitie and true Religion, bringeth honour to the King of Heaven." Most Englishmen, in fact, considered civility a precursor to religion. At the same time they feared its opposite, savagery, not only in Indians but potentially, too, in themselves. One of the principal arguments for establishing schools in Virginia was fear that otherwise the colonists or their posterity might "become utterly savage."

Blinded by ethnic arrogance and pious hopes, English observers misjudged Indian attitudes toward the colonists. Some spokesmen, such as Reverend Copland, simply read the wrong meaning into signs of hostility. As late as the eve of the massacre he thought that Powhatan and other chiefs moved inland because the Lord inspired them "to remoove from their owne warme and well seated and peopled habitations, to give place to Strangers. . . ." Most of Copland's contemporaries were less naive, but they too missed the implications of Indian animosity. Not until 1624 did the General Assembly concede that "we never perceaved that the natives of the Countrey did voluntarily yeeld them selves subjects to our gracyous Soveraigne, neither that they took any pride in that title, nor paide at any tyme any contrybutione of corne for sustentation of the Colony . . . but contrarily what at any time was done proceeded from feare and not love, and their corne procured by trade or the sworde." Even the company eventually admitted that the Indians attacked in 1622 because of "dayly feare" that the English would push them out of their lands altogether, much as the Spanish had done to the natives of the West Indies. Such candid admissions make clear that the Indians struck more out of fear and frustration than out of treachery.

A massacre might nonetheless have been avoided by a more realistic assessment of Indian strength. Until 1622 the colonists and their spokesmen at home agreed that the Indians "are neither strong nor many." A belief that they would succumb to a show of force was the basis for John Smith's policy, and its effectiveness was not lost on his successors. Nor could the lesson have been lost on the Indians. They quickly learned that the English had guns, ships, steel swords, and other weapons of war that made open resistance foolhardy. They also learned that the English kept coming in greater and greater numbers, especially after 1619, with consequent pressure on Indian lands and erosion of Indian culture. Moving forever westward could be one solution; succumbing to the intruders' insatiable demand for land, their demeaning treaties, and their insistence on social and religious transformation could be another. A third course lay in a desperate attempt to rid the Virginia coast of their presence. Given a severe enough thrashing the Englishmen might go away.

On Friday morning, 22 March 1622, many Indians came, as was their custom, to the scattered English plantations to barter furs and corn for imported goods. Some completed their trades, joined their hosts at breakfast, then slew them in cold blood. Other Indians, less patient, began the work of destruction on arrival. None were spared: women, children, workers in the field and in the shops. Most victims met death at the hands of old friends and by their own weapons, seized unexpectedly by the warriors and turned against their owners. Even the saintly George Thorpe, who had not long before killed some of the colony's mastiff dogs because they frightened the Indians, and who had built a handsome house for Opechancanough, fell victim to an Indian tomahawk. The Indians butchered his body as they did others, dragging portions off as trophies.

Before the day ended, three hundred forty-seven English lay dead. Most of the outlying plantations smoldered in ruins, strewn with mangled bodies and the remains of slaughtered farm animals. Jamestown and several other communities survived unscathed because of a last-minute warning from Christian Indians; a similar alert had failed to convince George Thorpe that treachery was afoot. At John Berkeley's plantation on Falling Creek, Berkeley and twenty-six of his people died; three miles away Thomas Sheffield and twelve others perished; seventeen fell at the college lands, ten at William Farrar's house, twelve at "Lieutenant Gibb's Dividend," six at Richard Owen's house including "One old Maid called blinde Margaret," while so many were slain at Martin's Hundred that some names were never recorded. Victims at almost thirty different localities included several members of the colony's council, though not John Rolfe, despite frequent assertions since that he met his death at Indian hands. (Rolfe did die in 1622, but had he fallen in the massacre the irony would not have been lost on the many chroniclers who reported the event; neither would his name have been absent from the musters of dead sent to the company.) But the peace that had been born with the Rolfe-Pocahontas marriage had most certainly died.

In mid-June *Seaflower* arrived in England with the chilling news. The London Company, even the Crown, could do little but offer advice and send additional supplies. The company quickly dispatched gunpowder and weapons, while King James contributed some old arms — "altogether unfitt, and of no use for moderne Service" — from the Tower of London. Not to be outdone, Captain John Smith volunteered to save the colony almost singlehandedly. Let the company, Smith pleaded, allow him "liberty and authority to make the best use I can of my experiences"; with one hundred soldiers and thirty sailors he would "inforce the Salvages to leave their Country, or bring them [into] feare and subjection. . . ." The London Company turned a deaf ear.

No Englishman, on either side of the Atlantic, doubted the fundamental course of action: the Indians, so recently friends, had become merciless enemies who must be totally destroyed. As one settler wrote home, "the Contrey is fullie determyned this Sommer to sett mainly upon th' Indians," and Governor Wyatt talked bluntly about "the extirpating of the Salvages." The company concurred. In October, 1622, it called for "a sharpe revenge uppon the bloody miscreantes, even to the measure that they intended against us, the rooting them out for being longer a people uppon the face of the Earth." Throughout the remainder of 1622 and well into 1623, armies of Englishmen relentlessly pursued the enemy, slaying hundreds and destroying villages and crops. The Indian warriors could not be crushed, however, for their mobility and knowledge of the terrain made direct assault on them impossible. The colonists soon resorted to more devious strategies. When efforts to poison Opechancanough failed, Captain William Tucker led twelve men to Pamunkey under pretense of making peace, then ambushed the natives, killing forty. Three of the victims proved to be chiefs, and for a while Opechancanough was believed to be one of them. But he survived to lead a later massacre. The settlers would not bring him to bay for another quarter century.

Not all the military initiative lay with the English. Knowing that the initial assault had stunned the colony, the Indians attacked stragglers and isolated settlements; English crops and cattle were destroyed or taken for Indian use. "Since the Massacre," Samuel Argall reported, "they have killed us in our owne doores, fields, and houses." Life and work went on for the survivors with a hoe in one hand, a gun or sword in the other.

The strain of living in constant insecurity combined with a severe shortage of food to bring the colonists' morale to a new low. Prices soared out of reach for all but the well-to-do: corn to 30s per bushel, meal to £12 sterling per hogshead, chickens to 15s. Hunting remained dangerous; only sizable parties could scout for game and they often used more time than the field work could spare, for new crops were essential to survival. Then disease took its frightful toll, and the death rate among those who escaped Indian arrows soon reached alarming proportions. Letters from the colony rang with plaintive cries for deliverance: "I am quite out of hart to live in this land[,] god send me well out of it"; "we lyve in the fearefullest age that ever christians lyved in"; "we are all undone." The population figures told a gruesome tale: pehaps 1000 settlers inhabited Virginia in 1619 and 3750 more came during the next three years; at the end of 1622 scarcely 2500 remained. The future of the colony, recently so promising, now seemed bleaker than ever. "The last massacre killed all our Countrie," wrote one survivor; "besides them they killed, they burst the heart of all the rest."

Death and discouragement struck not only the "old planters" and pre-1622 arrivals but post-massacre settlers as well, for surprisingly the company continued to find recruits willing to make the crossing. Some may have been aware of the hardships and gone with eyes open; most probably fell victim to the company's frantic efforts to prevent total disillusionment with the future of the colony. But whatever their expectations, the newcomers encountered perilous conditions. Lady Wyatt, a passenger to Virginia in 1623, recalled that "our Shipp was so . . . full of infection that after a while we saw little but throwing folkes over boord." Most of her fellow passengers died at sea or shortly after arrival. Governor Wyatt readily admitted "that great multitudes of new comers have been lost is not to be denied nor dissembled." He placed the blame partly on a shortage of beer, poultry, and meat, and partly on the climate which usually produced a burning fever during an immigrant's first summer. Newcomers indulged in intemperate consumption of water ("to plant a colony by water drinkers was an inexcusable error," the governor thought) that provoked serious intestinal disorders; death most often came in a relapse after the surgeon had bled his patient. In March 1623 George Sandys reported that since the massacre a "generall sickness" had taken almost 500 lives, "and not manie of the rest that have not knockt at the doores of death." The death toll for the years 1619–1625 may have reached 4500 persons out of perhaps 6500 who had been in Virginia during that period.

Enemies of the Sandys-Southampton party inevitably turned the appalling figures to their own political advantage. From its first year in office the new administration had claimed full credit for the colony's successes; now it had to account for overwhelming failure. Its strategy for defense was simple: blame everything on the massacre, and blame that in turn on perfidious Indians. Indeed, by casting all logic to the wind, the massacre might be portrayed as a blessing in disguise.

That, at any rate, was the objective of Edward Waterhouse. A member of the company, Waterhouse undertook in 1622 to write the latest in its periodic "declarations" on the state of the colony. The massacre could hardly be hidden; Waterhouse in fact set forth the most complete account of it. But he devoted as much or more space to repeating hackneyed praises of Virginia's soil and climate and to explaining away the recent disasters. Worse calamities, after all, had happened to the Spanish in their attempts to colonize America. Besides, Waterhouse insisted, "this Massacre must rather be beneficiall to the Plantation then impaire it." Why? "Because our hands which before were tied with gentlenesse and fair usage, are now set at liberty by the treacherous violence of the Savages . . . so that we, who hitherto have had possession of no more ground then their waste, and our purchase . . . may now by right of warre, and law of Nations, invade the Country, and destroy them who sought to destroy us. . . . Now their cleared grounds in all their villages (which are situate in the fruitfullest places of the land) shall be inhabited by us. . . ." Fortunately, contended Waterhouse, conquering the natives would prove easier than civilizing them, and of far greater advantage. They would no longer compete with the colonists for valuable wild game; and, as an added benefit, "the *Indians,* who before were used as friends, may now most justly be compelled to servitude and drudgery. . . ."

As Waterhouse's pamphlet revealed, the massacre of 1622 did not make the English abandon Virginia but it did sharply alter their attitudes toward the Indians. The earlier view that the natives were redeemable, both religiously and culturally, yielded to a belief that they were hopelessly debased. Plans for an Indian college were discarded and voices such as John Donne's and Patrick Copland's that had earlier pleaded for the wholesale conversion of the American natives fell silent. Even fundamental concern for Indian lives and property became a casualty. The year after the massacre Governor Wyatt announced that "Our first worke is expulsion of the Salvages to gaine the free range of the countrey for encrease of Cattle, swine etc. . . . for it is infinitely better to have no heathen among us, who at best were but as thornes in our sides, then to be at peace and league with them. . . ." Samuel Purchas agreed. The massacre, he argued, "hath now confiscated whatsoever remainders of right the unnaturall Naturalls had, and made both them and their Countrey wholly English. . . ."

Crown and company took a similar stance. In his pamphlet of 1622, designed primarily to tell Virginians how to raise silkworms and other agricultural crops, John Bonoeil voiced what had apparently become the official English viewpoint on the American Indian. Bonoeil's treatise had been published by authority of the company and carried endorsements from King James and the Earl of Southampton. Tucked away in the last part of the book, but conspicuous enough to have caught the eye of any reader, lurked an invitation to enslave the Indian remnant. "I utterly disclaime them," Bonoeil wrote, for they "know no industry, no Arts, no culture, nor no good use of this blessed Country heere, but are meere ignorance, sloth, and brutishnesse, and [are] an unprofitable burthen. . . . [They] are naturally borne slaves. . . . There is a naturall kind of right in you, that are bred noble, learned, wise, and vertuous, to direct them aright, to governe and to command them." Bonoeil's pamphlet, widely distributed in Virginia, was not publicly challenged. The subsequent record of Indian-white relations suggests that its message fell on receptive ears.

The massacre of 1622 shattered the colony and the Indian tribes; it fell lethally too on the London Company. The factional dispute that had preceded the shift in administrations in 1619 flared again in 1620, then lay relatively quiet until 1623. But the massacre and subsequent heavy mortality from famine and disease left the Sandys-Southampton party vulnerable to charges of mismanagement and gross incompetence. Open attacks on the company soon began to appear, instigated for the most part by Sir Thomas Smythe and his allies.

Unfortunately for the London Company, Sandys had a talent for making enemies. Beginning in 1618 and continuing until 1624, Sandys badgered Sir Thomas over the company's accounts for the years of Smythe's administration. Even some of Sandys' supporters became annoyed. He may have been right in suspecting the accounts, but Smythe had kept his records too laggardly for any thorough tally ever to be made. Haggling over them for six years merely rubbed salt into old wounds. Time and again Sandys' love for the company and his determination to make it succeed caused him to push some projects past the breaking point. His frantic efforts to increase the population of the colony, despite inadequate provisions and facilities there (both before and after the massacre), as well as his excessively persistent investigation of Smythe's accounts, showed his misguided zeal.

Still another example is Sandys' efforts to free the company of any taint of piracy. Robert Rich, second Earl of Warwick and leader of a clan of influential aristocrats, relished quasi-legal ventures on the high seas. Raiding Spanish vessels had been almost a national mania under Queen Elizabeth and lingered into the seventeenth century as an important stimulus to English nationalism. But the official termination of warfare with Spain in 1604, and King James' rather cordial attitude toward Madrid, had compelled English corsairs to invent subterfuges for their attacks on the ships and territories of His Most Catholic Majesty. Warwick found a way. He secured from the King of England a license to capture pirates; he could then dispatch his ships fully armed and geared for battle. He also obtained a commission from the Duke of Savoy, then at odds with Spain, which provided him at least a paper excuse for preying on Spanish vessels. And so the Rich family sent ships to the Indian Ocean and to the Caribbean, where opportunities for plunder were rife. One of Warwick's vessels, *Treasurer,* under Captain Daniel Elfrith, landed at Jamestown in 1618; there Samuel Argall, himself a part owner of the ship, refitted it for a cruise in the West Indies. Within a few months it was back in Jamestown with a cargo of Negroes and other contraband. Sir George Yeardley, who had in the meantime succeeded Argall as Governor, refused to let *Treasurer* barter its wares and on orders from Sandys prepared to seize it. Captain Elfrith eventually disposed of his cargo in Bermuda.

Sandys insisted on thwarting Warwick's piratical efforts from London as vigorously as Yeardley had from Virginia, even though the earl was an ally in the struggle of 1619 against Sir Thomas Smythe and a powerful force both in the company and in the halls of Westminster. Sandys rightly feared that Warwick's international machinations might cast a shadow over the company; he wrongly (so far as the health of the company was concerned) prosecuted everyone involved on Warwick's side.

First to feel Sandys' wrath was Argall, by then back in England, who was charged with aiding and abetting the pirates and with other infractions. Next, Sandys accused Captain Butler, Governor of Bermuda at the time *Treasurer* arrived there, of inviting Spanish reprisals by entertaining looters of Spanish ships. ("By what spirit of devination" Butler replied with considerable logic, "I should take him for a pirate who had as lawful a commission . . . as these talkative tedious orators . . . ?") The Rich family protected Argall and Butler from legal prosecution, thus thwarting Sandys, but neither man could thereafter be counted a friend of the London Company. On his next visit to Virginia, Butler gathered damning evidence for a report on "The Unmasked Face of our Colony of Virginia as it was in the Winter of the yeare 1622." His diatribe claimed that the plantations were "seated uppon meer Salt Marishes full of infectious Boggs and muddy Creeks"; that the people had to wade into water in the wintertime to unload ships "& therby gett . . . vyolent surfeits of

Cold upon Cold"; that no guest houses existed for new arrivals who "are not only seen dyinge under hedges and in the woods, but beinge dead ly some of them for many dayes unregarded and unburied." Virginia's houses, Butler insisted, were worse than any in England; the plantation without fortifications; the iron and glass works in shambles, with tobacco the only surviving business and "every man madded upon that"; while the government he termed ignorant and unjust. Without immediate reform by "some divine and supreame hand," Butler predicted, "in steed of a Plantacion itt will shortly gett the name of a slaughter house."

The "divine and supreame hand" Butler had in mind, or at least that lurked in the minds of his friends in London, was King James. Because voting by person rather than by shares prevailed at the company's General Courts, Sandys could usually win crucial challenges to his power by corralling new stockholders; they would collectively hold few shares but could outvote his wealthier though less numerous opponents. Not for nothing had Sandys earned a reputation as an astute Parliamentarian. In desperation Smythe's backers turned to the royal court: if they couldn't wrest control from Sandys, they might at least take the company away from him. James had already begun to view the company as "a seminary for a seditious parliament." A petition to the King in the spring of 1623 therefore requested a royal investigation.

In mid-April both sides to the dispute stated their cases to the Privy Council. Charges and counter-charges, hurled with "much heat and bitterness," turned the proceedings into near bedlam. John Chamberlain notified Sir Dudley Carleton that Sir Edward Sackville of the Sandys party "carried himself so malapertly and insolently that the King was faine to take him downe soundly and roundly. . . . " The King could restore good behavior in his presence, but he could not prevent outbursts of animosity away from court. The company's factions, Chamberlain observed, "are growne so violent . . . they seldom meet upon the Exchange or in the streets but they brabble and quarrell, so that if that societie be not dissolved the sooner, or cast in a new mould, worse effects may follow then the whole business is worth."

By that time the search for a "new mould" was well under-way. In May the Privy Council appointed an impartial commission to investigate the entire career of the London Company and its interconnected Bermuda Company; in the meantime the colonies would be under the direct control of the Crown. Sir William Jones, Justice of the Court of Common Pleas, served as chairman of the commission. The six other members were all prominent gentlemen.

In many respects the findings of the Jones Commission were a foregone conclusion. The company had meant well; it had tried for a decade and a half to bring peace and prosperity to the colonists, honor and glory to the empire, and where possible, profits to itself. But it had failed. The colonists now languished ill-housed, ill-fed, surrounded by an embittered and implacable enemy, and with little hope for better times without hefty infusions of money and wise leadership. In both commodities the London Company was bankrupt.

Under the skillful direction of Nathaniel Rich, the Smythe-Warwick faction presented a convincing case against the Sandys administration. There could be no hiding the "miserable and most desperate estate" of the colony, nor the appalling mortality rate that by 1624 amounted to perhaps sixty-five percent of all persons who had been in Virginia in 1619 or gone there since. And the company had no funds with which to bail out the colony. The money raised from the sale of stock, from tobacco and other commodities, and from the lottery had been spent on ships, supplies, and on setting up iron, glass, and silk works. Total expenditures for the first four years under Sandys and Southampton reached approximately £90,000; iron alone had taken £5000. After the disasters of 1622–1623, no new investors could be found. Only the royal treasury could salvage the floundering colony.

That was the opinion of, among others, Captain John

Smith. He watched the proceedings with extreme interest and took perverse satisfaction in the fall of those who had scorned his own efforts. His *Generall Historie,* published in 1624 but much of it written while the investigation was underway, suggested that "if you please to compare what hath beene spent, sent, discovered, and done this fifteene yeares, by that we did in the first three yeares . . . you may easily finde what hath beene the cause of those disasters in *Virginia.*"

A page later Smith entered what for him must have been a gratifying chore, his answers to seven questions put to him by "his Majesties Commissioners for the reformation of *Virginia.*" The old warrior had been asked, at last, for his opinions on the past, present, and future of the colony, matters on which Smith had never been reluctant to offer gratuitous advice. The very phrasing of the first question must have warmed his heart (though we have it only from Smith's account which may reflect the way he *wished* the question had been worded) : *"What conceive you is the cause the Plantation hath prospered no better since you left it in so good a forwardnesse?"* Smith's answer: "Idlenesse and carelessnesse. . . ." To the commissioners' second question, why nothing but tobacco comes out of so fertile a country, Smith suggested a two-fold explanation: frequent changes in governors and pricing tobacco higher than corn. And in good military tradition Smith replied to a question about the causes of the massacre by decrying a lack of martial discipline, excessive dispersal of plantations, and the irresponsible employment of Indians as "Fowlers and Huntsmen" with English weapons. "In my time," Smith recalled, ". . . it was death to him that should shew a Salvage the use of a Peece."

Captain Smith saw abundant faults in the present state of both colony and company, and although he made no startlingly original observations, his report reflected a deep understanding of the process of colonization. Smith saw the complexity of the situation. "The multiplicity of opinions here, and Officers there," he considered a basic flaw. Of equal magnitude was the hiring at fixed rates of private ships to transport men and materials to the colony. At £6 per passenger and £3 per ton of goods, Smith contended, shipmasters crowded their vessels past the safety point; "sicknesse, diseases, and mortality," resulted. At fault too were the letters and reports from Virginia that painted the conditions of the colony in unrealistic hues, leading readers at home to believe "that all things were wel, to which error here they have beene ever much subject." Moreover, many adventurers simply didn't care about the fate of the colony, their great estates easily absorbing whatever loss they incurred. After all, a mere £12.10 invested now earned its owner a share equal to that of any original investor or settler who staked his life and fortune in the colony. Smith's bitterness crept through many of his answers to the commissioners.

At bottom, though, John Smith blamed the company. He carefully avoided naming any culprits: "grosse errors have beene committed," but "I have no leisure to looke into any mans particular. . . ." The whole company had badly failed the colony. The officers in England, Smith noted, did not go bankrupt or seek relief from their places; those in Virginia did both. Some in the company, out of covetousness and extortion, controlled the goods sent to Virginia and sold them at exorbitant rates. Avaricious ship captains raised the price of servants to forty or sixty pounds who had been sent out by the company for ten. The cure for all these ills, according to Captain Smith, depended on royal control, or at least royal assistance. The heads of colony and company should account annually to the Crown or some impartial body. Returning to an old theme, Smith especially stressed the need for good workmen, "not such delinquents as here cannot be ruled by all the lawes in *England* . . . [;] to rectify a commonwealth with debaushed people is impossible. . . ." Virginia, he reminded the commissioners, "is no Country to pillage as the Romans found: all you expect from thence must be by labour."

To meet the colony's fiscal problems, Smith advocated a poll tax of a penny per person throughout the King's dominions or two pence on every chimney, or the like, to be used for shipping good servants and others to the New World. They, in turn, would be Virginians, with no obligation but loyalty to the Crown of England. Men would then go willingly and the colony would soon prosper. As for the company's patent, the King might as well take it from those who now had it; they promised great things and belittled Smith and the other early leaders, but "it is not likely we could have done much worse."

There is no evidence of how seriously the Jones Commission took Smith's advice. His low opinion of the company corroborated other testimony, and he was, after all, one of the best informed men in all England, perhaps in the world, on the practical aspects of colonization. The commissioners knew that he had played a leading role in the first permanent English outpost in America, had experienced a wide range of dealings with the Indians, had explored and mapped much of the British sector, and had published hundreds of pages of colonization literature. They also knew that he was vain, excessively sensitive about his own reputation, and a bit of a braggart. But he was the only governor of early Virginia to have left the colony in better condition than he found it. It is perhaps not coincidental then that the initial proposal of the Privy Council, on recommendation of the Jones Commission, called for the surrender of the charter of 1612 and its replacement by a new one modelled along the lines of the charter of 1606. This is what Smith seems to have advocated, and it might have saved the company from extinction.

But the company would have none of it. On 20 October 1623 the Sandys party in General Court rejected the Privy Council's proposal. The government now had no recourse but to cancel the charter unilaterally, and it immediately began *quo warranto* proceedings. After several months of legal process, the Court of King's Bench on 24 May 1624 officially recalled the charter. The London Company was dead.

ELIZABETHA REGINA · Virginia · IACOBVS · REX · Now Planted · CAROLVS · PRINCEPS

Ould · Virginia · C. Henri · Nett · England ·
C. Fear · C. Chareis · B. la Ware · Renolds · Anne · C. Elizabeth
Hatoraſk · C. James · Richmond
Willowbyes Ila.

Pembruk CB.

THE
GENERALL HISTORIE
OF
Virginia, New-England, and the Summer
Iſles: with the names of the Adventurers,
Planters, and Governours from their
firſt beginning An: 1584. to this
preſent 1624.

With the Procedings of thoſe Severall Colonies
and the Accidents that befell them in all their
Journyes and Diſcoveries.

Alſo the Maps and Deſcriptions of all thoſe
Countryes, their Commodities, people,
Government, Cuſtomes, and Religion
yet knowne.

DIVIDED INTO SIXE BOOKES.

By Captane IOHN SMITH ſometymes Governour
in theſe Countryes & Admirall
of New England.

LONDON.
Printed by I.D. and
I.H. for Michael
Sparkes.
1624.

VIRGINIA
EN DAT · QVINTVM

COGNITA MIHI
GENS INC. · SERVIET

The title page of Smith's most influential book

X
"Still Breathing Virginia"

JOHN SMITH felt no remorse at the company's demise. It had, he believed, treated him badly and served his colony poorly. The Smythe administration had failed to support his policies or supply him adequately; the Sandys-Southampton administration had ignored him completely. Yet with the dissolution of the company Smith lost his best hope for returning to America. Lacking substantial influence with the Crown or with private promoters, and too poor to finance his own expeditions, after 1624 Captain Smith forsook his dreams of rescuing Virginia by new acts of heroism and leadership. Reluctantly, but energetically, he searched for other ways to further the settlement of America.

For a while Smith hoped New England might provide the opportunities prematurely closed to him in Virginia. But Virginia's failures now hampered efforts in New England; few investors wanted to risk a repetition of the disasters that had struck the Jamestown colony. Smith, of course, remained supremely confident that he could establish a successful colony in New England. He knew the land, the natives, the problems, and thanks to his experiences in Virginia, he knew the solutions. But unfortunately for his own prospects he had already set forth much of that knowledge in his writings. Hence the small band of religious dissenters, later dubbed "Pilgrims," that set sail for America in the fall of 1620 found it cheaper to buy his books than to hire him, or so Smith claimed. (A valid claim it appears: Elder Brewster of the Pilgrims owned a copy of the *Description of New England,* and Governor Bradford's history referred to Smith's map.) Before John Smith's life ended, larger and better-prepared ventures established other outposts in New England, and they too saved money by using Smith's works instead of the captain himself. Besides, Smith's religious orthodoxy considerably diminished his appeal to colonists of Puritan proclivities. Landbound in England, he waited fretfully for a new chance to use his experience.

Smith's interest in New England stemmed not only from his conviction that England's future lay in American colonization, but also from a pressing need for employment. As heir to his father's lands in Lincolnshire, John Smith enjoyed a fairly regular but extremely modest income from rentals. He had received no remuneration from the London Company, outside of his upkeep in Virginia, and no answer to his appeal of 1621 for some tangible recognition of his services to the Jamestown colony. The company's minutes record that "Captain John Smith in his peticion sheweth that . . . he hath . . . adventured money for the good of the Plantacion and twise built James Towne and fower other perticuler Plantacions . . . and relieved the Colony willingly three yeares with that which he gott from the Savages with great perill and hazard of his life. . . ." His petition was shunted off to "the Committee appointed for rewarding of men upon merrites," which apparently thought his service deserved no reward.

Smith fared no better with the merchant guilds during the early 1620s. The Worshipful Company of Fishmongers was unimpressed by the captain's plea that his project for overseas fishing would be "wonderfull, beneficiall and gaynefull to this Kingdome." Equally unimpressed were the other companies — some thirty of them — that Smith solicited in person or through inscribed copies of his writings. Little wonder that during these frustrating years he frequently complained of poverty and ingratitude. He was spending his own money to promote colonization but receiving nothing in return. "I never had power and meanes to do any thing . . . but in such a penurious and miserable maner," he lamented in 1620, "as if I had gone a begging to builde an University . . . [B]etwixt the spurre of Desire, and the bridle of Reason, I am neare ridden to death in a ring of Despaire."

Increasingly John Smith knew moments of discouragement and self-pity. Still, the man had too much courage to stay inactive or even depressed for long. "Vincere est vivere" read the motto on his hard-won coat of arms, and for Smith "to conquer is to live" meant overcoming adversity as well as enemies. By 1622 — the year of the massacre in Virginia and a time of mounting disappointments in his quest for an active role in America — the captain's morale had regained some of its natural buoyancy. He had lost heavily in time and money, he complained in the revised edition of *New Englands Trials,* but he believed as much as ever in the future of the colonies. He believed too in the rightness of his loyalty to them, "for they have bin my wife, my hawks, my hounds, my cards, my dice, and in totall my best content. . . . [W]ere there not one English man remaining (as God be thanked there is some thousands) I would yet begin againe with as small meanes as I did at the first."

For many years John Smith had compensated for his lack of physical involvement in colonization by serving as its chief publicist. His earlier books had earned some acclaim, though his own haste, combined with his inexperience as a writer, had produced chronicles rather than connected narratives. Now, during the final decade of his life, John Smith wrote with renewed gusto and with increased skill. He never became a literary craftsman, and he continued to borrow heavily from his own and others' works, but as the 1620s wore on Captain John Smith became recognized as one of the major historians of his day. Publication thus served as Smith's contribution to the English conquest of America as well as an outlet for his own frustration.

Two themes dominated his writing: the glorious future of British America that awaited only wise government and industrious settlers, and the need to learn from the experience of earlier colonies — Spanish, Portuguese, French, as well as English. The emphasis on experience had implicit, and often explicit, application to his own potential role in America. Again and again he pointed out that colonization of a new continent had no infallible precedents; only by hard work and direct experience could the right methods be found to extend the English empire to America. "But it is not a worke for every one to manage such an affaire," Smith warned, "as [to] make a discovery and plant a colony, it requires all the best parts of art, judgement, courage, honesty, constancy, diligence, and industry, to do but neere well." Smith never doubted that he possessed those qualities and that *his* experience should be the catalyst to success. Nor did he doubt the value of the New World. He had been in Africa, Asia, Europe, and America, and of all he considered America "the fittest place for an earthly Paradise." That remained an overriding theme of his *Map of Virginia* (1612), his *Description of New England* (1616), and his *New Englands Trials* (1620, 1622). And in 1624 it reappeared as the dominant thrust of *The Generall Historie of Virginia, New-England, and the Summer Isles,* his largest and most influential book.

At a meeting of the stockholders of the London Company on 12 April 1621, John Smyth of Nibley, Gloustershire, moved that Virginia's prestige among "Common Subjectes" be raised by publication of "a faire & perspicuous history . . . of that Country, from her first discovery to this day." Smyth's audience responded with "a very great applause." Soon after, Captain John Smith decided that he should be the author. Encouragement may have come from Samuel Purchas or from others who knew his earlier writings on the colonies, or he may merely have felt compelled to tell the story before someone beat him to it. In any event, Smith now gave all his attention to a comprehensive history of British America.

He worked rapidly and finished the first part within a year. But as the manuscript neared completion in 1623 it ran headlong into the troubles of the London Company which declined to increase its debts by printing an expensive book — whatever its obligation to the author may have been. John Smith insisted that "in the Companies name I was requested to doe it," but the request, if ever made, must have been unofficial. The controlling faction would not have been likely to support publication under any circumstances, because of Smith's candid criticism and his lack of influence with Southamptom and Sandys; faced with financial collapse and the imminent loss of its charter, the company could have had little interest in such a project. Smith therefore turned to private patronage.

"These observations are all I have for the expenses of a thousand pound, and the losse of eighteene yeeres of time, besides all the travels, dangers, miseries & incumbrances for my countries good, I have endured *Gratis*," Smith explained in a prospectus issued late in 1623. He urged public-minded donors to contribute the £100 necessary to put his book in print. In the end it took only one donor: Frances, Duchess of Richmond and Lenox (the "double duchess" she was often called), a relative of the King by marriage and one of the wealthiest women in England. Her largess permitted the book to be registered with the Stationer's Company on 12 July 1624, after hasty manufacture by two separate trade printers, John Dawson and John Haviland. Smith gratefully acknowledged his benefactress in an Epistle Dedicatory, adding Lady Frances to his other women saviors — "the beauteous Lady *Tragabigzanda*," "the charitable Lady *Callamata*," "that blessed *Pokahontas*," and "the good Lady *Madam Chanoyes*" — for without the help of the Duchess, he confessed, his book would have "dyed in the wombe."

Like Smith's earlier writings, the *Generall Historie* followed the nationalistic tradition of Hakluyt and Purchas: it sought to inspire all Britons to join cause for the glory of the empire. Smith had stated the case as early as 1616: "So that the busi-

nesse prosper, I have my desire; be it by *Londoner, Scot,*
Welch, or *English,* that are true subjects to our King and
Countrey[,] . . . there is more then enough for all, if they
could bee content but to proceed." To encourage further
interest and investment in colonization Captain Smith now set
forth Britain's accomplishments in Virginia, Bermuda, and
New England, with an implicit exhortation to learn from past
mistakes. According to his prospectus, his story should "stirre
up a double new life in the Adventurers, when they shall see
plainely the causes of all those defailments, and how they may
be amended." The *Generall Historie* stressed once again the
importance of honest and efficient government, adequate
planning, diligent settlers, and active aid from the Crown;
England's future in the New World awaited only firm leadership and enthusiastic public support.

To get that message across, Smith attempted a work of
unprecedented scope: the whole sweep of English America
from the discoveries of John Cabot in 1497 to the eve of
publication in 1624. Within a volume of nearly two hundred
fifty folio pages, he presented the story of England's efforts to
plant in the American wilderness the seeds of a new England.
Without the distracting tales of voyages to Russia, Africa, and
the Far East that encumbered the pages of Hakluyt's and
Purchas' works, and without the narrow perspective that
characterized most of England's New World reportage, Smith
was free to examine all phases of the American project.

He divided his work into six books. The first summarized
England's contact with America before 1607; the second reprinted the section of his *Map of Virginia* that described the
natives, including a brief vocabulary for readers who "doe
desire to know the manner of their Language"; Books III and
IV treated Virginia from 1607 to 1624; Book V recounted the
history of Bermuda, drawn largely from a manuscript by
former governor Nathaniel Butler; and the concluding book
reprinted and expanded Smith's *Description of New England.*

The most original part of the *Generall Historie* appeared in the third book. There Smith added almost ten thousand words to extracts from his earlier publications on Virginia. Much of the new writing concerned Indian affairs — a popular topic since the recent massacre, and one on which Smith liked to lecture his countrymen. He had dealt with the natives firmly, he insisted; mollycoddling by Newport and subsequent leaders had brought catastrophe. Only an expanded account of his rescue by Pocahontas softened Smith's picture of Indian-white relations. Nothing, however, ameliorated his aspersions on the company and on his particular enemies. Smith reviewed the rise and fall of the London Company and pointed an accusing finger at those who had thwarted his efforts or ignored his advice. A tone of wounded pride infuses Book III and continues into Book IV where Smith focused on events in the colony after his departure. For Smith, writing the *Generall Historie* had been part craftsmanship, part catharsis.

Smith's magnum opus conformed to the Hakluyt-Purchas model in method as well as theme. He denied being a "Compiler by hearsay," but in truth the *Generall Historie* owed almost as much to Smith's fellow chroniclers as it did to the Duchess of Richmond and Lenox; while she provided the cash, they provided much of the contents. Throughout major portions of the book, Smith compiled and edited rather than authored, usually giving credit where appropriate, but sometimes not. He did not intend to deceive; the literary canons of his day condoned such eclectic borrowing, and Smith was more conscientious with credit lines than most of his contemporaries. But much of his *Generall Historie* is second-hand, and much of it lacks clarity if not coherence. Nor was the book a stylistic masterpiece. As he himself admitted in the dedicatory preface to Lady Frances, his story "ought to have been clad in better robes than my rude military hand can cut out in Paper Ornaments. But because, of the most things therein I . . . have beene a reall Actor; I take myself to have a property in them: and therefore have been bold to challenge them to come under the reach of my owne rough Pen."

Smith embellished his text with numerous illustrations. Four large maps, each adorned with appropriate pictures, showed the coastlines and principal landmarks of the Roanoke area, Virginia, Bermuda, and New England. In appreciation of the Duchess's assistance, Smith inserted her portrait as a frontispiece. Smaller likenesses of England's past, present, and future monarchs — Elizabeth, James, and Charles — graced the title page, which included as backdrop a panoply of maps, American Indian vignettes, and coats of arms. Smith's armorial insignia, with its three Turks' heads, received a prominent position.

The captain's vanity fared as well in the pictorial displays. A two-page spread between Books I and II revealed Smith in a variety of dramatic situations: captured by the Indians in 1607, saved from execution by Pocahontas, and (in two separate scenes) singlehandedly overpowering Indian chieftains. Between Books V and VI appeared a map of the New England coast, reengraved from the *Description of New England,* with a handsome likeness of the author in the upper left corner. Beneath the portrait appeared a brief verse by John Davies, one of England's better poets, that would have made a more modest man blush:

> These are the lines that shew thy Face; but those
> That shew thy Grace and Glory, brighter bee:
> Thy Faire-Discoveries and Fowle-Overthrowes
> Of Salvages, much Civilliz'd by thee
> Best shew thy Spirit; and to it Glory Wyn;
> So, thou art Brasse without, but Golde within.

Such lines, along with a score of lavishly complimentary poems interspersed through the volume — written by such friends as Samuel Purchas, Richard Gunnell, and Ralegh Crashaw — suggest that Smith had one eye on the future of Virginia, the other on his own reputation. But if he gave more credit to himself than to others, and if he admonished as much as he praised, he could be forgiven. Widely read and frequently reprinted, the *Generall Historie* filled England's need for an epic account of the island nation's efforts to conquer a continent.

To encourage prospective investors to read his book, Smith contributed copies of "this Cronologicall discourse" to several of London's powerful craftsmen's guilds, many of which had already invested heavily in the Virginia venture, and which might still be persuaded to support the captain's colonizing schemes. To the Society of Cordwainers he made his usual pitch: only the "ill managdging" of the colony had kept them and others from profiting in the enterprise, "the Causes thereof you may reade at Large in this Booke." His flyleaf inscription on a presentation copy to the cordwainers concluded with the hope that they "give it Lodging in your Hall freelie to be perused for ever, in memorie of your Noblenesse towards mee. . . ." Through such efforts to circulate his books Smith continued to promote English colonization, a fact well recognized by Reverend Samuel Purchas, whose *Hakluytus posthumus, or Purchas his pilgrimes,* published in 1625, drew on the *Generall Historie.* "That industrious Gentleman Captaine John Smith," Purchas noted, was "still breathing Virginia, and diligent [in his] enquiry and writing . . . for seeing he cannot there be employed to performe Virginian exploits worthy the writing, here he employeth himselfe to write Virginian affaires worthy the reading. . . ."

Such praise must have raised the captain's sagging spirits. It probably did little, however, for his pocketbook, and a proud man could not depend forever on the generosity of wealthy friends. But now Smith had a literary reputation and could try his hand at something more lucrative and less expensive to produce, something without costly illustrations and fancy typography, something practical and saleable. In 1625 a prolific though often superficial writer named Gervase Markham had published *The Soldier's Accidence,* a primer on military procedures. Markham had no claim to military expertise; Smith had a little to seamanship, so it was at least as fitting that Smith in 1626 should produce the naval counterpart, *An*

Accidence for young Sea-men: or Their Path-way to Experience. Nothing comparable on the subject existed in the English language, so the field lay open for a brief and explicit manual.

With no competition and with a naval war against Spain recently begun, Smith's treatise could hardly miss. *The Accidence* sold well enough to justify a second edition in 1627 and a greatly expanded version, entitled *A Sea Grammar,* that same year. It too drew on Markham's example: the year before he had written *The Soldier's Grammar.* Smith also leaned heavily on Sir Henry Mainwaring's *Seaman's Dictionary,* previously written but not printed until 1644, which the captain somehow obtained in manuscript. But unlike Markham and Mainwaring, Smith had a larger purpose than mere profit or explication, for even in his guide for seamen John Smith promoted English colonization. The opening note in *The Accidence* dwelled more on settlement than on seamanship; colonization also crept into most of the laudatory poems that prefaced the *Sea Grammar* and into the examples and admonitions of both volumes.

Smith's manual on seamanship went through several editions during the seventeenth century, but it was not Smith's natural genre. More to his liking, no doubt, and more in keeping with his obsessive need to praise British America were *The True Travels, Adventures, and Observations of Captaine John Smith, in Europe, Asia, Affrica, and America, from Anno Domini 1593 to 1629,* published in 1630. This was Smith's chance to record his adventures before the Virginia years, to bring attention to the events that had once been the high points of his life but which had received scant public attention. In 1625 Samuel Purchas had published an extract from a book attributed to Francisco Ferneza, secretary to Zsigmond Bathory, that recounted Smith's Hungarian deeds. Sir Robert Cotton, a distinguished antiquarian and book collector, then urged the captain to write his autobiography. Smith was in the right mood: by 1628 he was taking such pride in the earlier part of his career that he signed a commendatory verse in a friend's book, *"Captaine* John Smith — 'Hungariensis.' " For a brief moment, Smith of Hungary overshadowed Smith of Jamestown.

But not for long. Although part one of *True Travels* related Smith's European and Asian exploits from 1593 to 1604, the second part, comprising more than one third of the text, returned to the familiar topic of British exploration and colonization. Here Smith discussed English voyages to Guiana, the Amazon River, and the West Indies. He also seized the opportunity to bring his readers up-to-date on developments in Virginia, Bermuda, and New England since publication of his *Generall Historie.*

Smith relished inclusion of the section on Virginia, for the colony's remarkable revival in five years of royal control seemed to vindicate his years of admonition and advice. King James had died shortly after the revocation of the London Company's charter; his successor, Charles I, had decreed that "the Governement of the Collonie of *Virginia,* shall ymediately depend uppon Our Selfe, and not be commyted to anie Companie or Corporation." Accordingly, a series of Crown-appointed governors — Sir Francis Wyatt until 1626, Sir George Yeardley again for the next two years, and Sir John Harvey after 1628 — ruled the colony. They provided relatively stable and energetic government, with the assistance of an eleven-man council and the Assembly, though the role of the latter body remained imprecise. In other ways, too, the colony improved. Termination of the self-seeking London Company had freed commerce with the mother country; Smith rejoiced that "there have gone so many voluntarie ships within this two yeeres [1625–1627], as have furnished them with Apparell, Sacke, *Aquavitae,* and all necessaries, much better than ever before." The colonists were now adequately armed, and a general peace prevailed with the Indians. Tobacco flourished but so did corn; the colony no longer depended on purchases from the Indians or on shipments from

England. New houses provided comfortable shelter, and by cutting down many of the tall trees the settlers had let the sun dry much of the swampy ground. Virginia was now "much more healthfull than before . . . , few Countreyes are lesse troubled with death, sicknesse, or any other disease. . . ." Smith chided the new era in Virginia only for its lack of discoveries. "He is a great traveller," Smith reported sarcastically, "that hath gone up and downe the river of *James Towne,* been at *Pamaunke, Smiths* Isles, or *Accomack.*" "For Discoveries they have made none. . . ." Virginia still needed John Smith.

The captain was almost as satisfied with New England's promise as with Virginia's revival. The Plymouth Colony, despite some cruel years and its rejection of Smith's guiding hand (for which, he insisted, they "payed soundly in trying their selfe-willed conclusions") now prospered. Still another promising beginning had been made in 1629 when "a great company of people of good ranke, zeal, meanes, and quality" founded a new outpost on Massachusetts Bay. The aging warrior took obvious pride in reporting the improved health of "those Countries Captaine *Smith* oft times used to call his children. . . ."

During the 1620s John Smith spent most of his time in London. The great city bustled with activity, something he had always needed; there too he had access to the printers and engravers who could transform his barely legible manuscripts into marketable books. Those books in turn brought Captain Smith some of the prestige and acclaim he had long craved. With the death of Hakluyt in 1616, of Ralegh (by execution) in 1618, and of Purchas in 1626, Smith became England's foremost champion of colonization and its most prominent historian. Ben Jonson, then at the height of his career, quoted Smith in one of his plays, and Richard Gunnell, a leading theatrical producer, devoted at least part of a script to the captain's adventures. Purchas, of course, had often praised him. London knew John Smith well.

The city also offered a chance to be near friends. He had never married, had few close relatives, and eschewed frivolous pastimes. (According to a comrade in the Hungarian campaign: "I never knew a Warryer yet, but thee / From wine, tobacco, debts, dice, oaths so free.") Because he had become a gentleman and something of a celebrity, Smith maintained a style he could barely afford. He probably kept a room at one of the inns, and he may at times have lodged at the London home of Lord Willoughby. Toward the end of the decade he is known to have lived for a while with Sir Samuel Saltonstall, a cousin of one of the early settlers of Massachusetts, in St. Sepulchre's Parish. But Smith was not city-bound. He travelled widely, for his circle of acquaintances now reached from the Bertie family and other childhood friends in eastern Lincolnshire to Sir Humphrey Mildmay in Essex and prosperous merchants in the West Country. The chance to visit friends brought solace and at the same time eased Smith's financial burdens.

It was at the home of Humphrey Mildmay in Danbury, Essex, that Captain John Smith penned his last tribute to British America. It reflected the best of Smith — his deep concern for England's place in the world; his conviction that experience must be the ultimate teacher; his profound commitment to the colonies' welfare. Smith's last work also showed him at his worst: his craving for recognition as a major colonizer, his almost paranoid belief that enemies conspired to thwart him, his pathetic repetition of events that cast him in heroic light. But in its strengths and weaknesses, *Avertisements for the unexperienced Planters of New-England or any where* was an appropriate climax to Smith's career as a leading publicist of English colonization. "I have not been more willing, at the request of my friends to print this discourse," Smith wrote, "than I am ready to live and dye among you . . . and [to make] *Virginia* and *New-England,* my heires, executors, administrators and assignes."

Smith had written most, if not all, of the *Advertisements* by October 1630, although it did not go on sale at Robert Milbourne's shop in St. Paul's churchyard until the next year. Publication may have been slowed by ill health, for in June of 1631 John Smith, too weak to sign his name, scrawled his mark on a last will and testament in which he acknowledged that he was "sicke in body, but of perfect mynde and memory." But his bodily ailments, if in fact they slowed his writing, failed to dull the vigor and enthusiasm of his prose.

Nor did they dim Smith's persistent optimism. He was always ready to fault the inept management of England's colonies; at the same time he never ceased to laud their potential. Now, in his last public assessment of British America, he could point to actual as well as latent achievements. After making clear his lack of sympathy with theology of the Separatists and Congregationalists of New England, Smith praised their leaders and followers who were, he thought, "much more fit for such a businesse, and better furnished of all necessaries if they arrive well, than was ever any Plantation went out of *England.*" Smith also contrasted the New Englanders' relative autonomy under a royal charter with Virginia's long subservience to a distant and ill-informed company that exploited its colony, assuming that "all the world was Oatmeale there." At last the right lessons of the Jamestown experiment were taking hold. Colonization would now flourish under competent leaders, zealous settlers, and self-governing plantations. The ill-fated attempts at Roanoke and Sagadahoc and the ill-managed foothold at Jamestown had finally been succeeded by wisely managed and properly manned undertakings at Plymouth and Massachusetts Bay, and by a thoroughly revamped effort in Virginia.

Had he lived another two decades Smith would have had further cause for pride. Virginia continued to thrive despite another massacre by Opechancanough's warriors and a continuing mania for tobacco. In most matters Virginia substantially fulfilled the captain's hopes: in its swelling and increasingly industrious population, its mounting prosperity, its growing social and political stability. New England would have pleased him too, despite its religious aberrations, for by mid-century the plantation at Massachusetts Bay had expanded amazingly and had been augmented by new settlements at Connecticut, Rhode Island, and New Haven. Still other colonies had been established in Maryland, across Chesapeake Bay from Virginia, and on several Caribbean islands. The survival of British America, uncertain since the days of Richard Hakluyt and Sir Walter Ralegh, was assured. John Smith had made his point.

He did not, however, live to see his ideas spread and prosper along the full span of eastern North America. The observation in his *Generall Historie* applied to himself as well as to the early career of England's colonies: "can we not but lament, it was our fortunes to end when we had but onely learned how to begin, and found the right course how to proceed." Smith's end came just as England found the right course. On 21 June 1631, the day he dictated his will, the man who had survived countless battles on four continents, who had withstood a harrowing succession of wounds, poisonings, shipwrecks, and captivities, died in his bed. He had lived for slightly more than half a century, a half-century of momentous drama and change in the history of England and in the history of the world. Throughout he epitomized his era as did few of his contemporaries. And he could take pride in having won fame by his own merits. He rose from humble origins in an age when society's barriers were seldom breached; with indomitable will and energy he achieved prominence and social esteem. Moreover, he left a lasting contribution to his nation and to his age, for more than any other man or woman John Smith made British America a reality — a fact clear from the perspective of three and a half centuries and one that many of his contemporaries understood as well.

After his friends laid the captain's body to rest in St. Sepulchre's Church, lest anyone forget the man or his deeds they placed a memorial tablet on the wall. It reads in part:

> Here lies one conquer'd that hath conquer'd Kings,
> Subdu'd large Territories, and done things
> Which to the World impossible would seeme,
> But that the truth is held in more esteeme.
>
> Shall I report his former service done
> In honour of his God and Christendome;
> How that he did divide from Pagans three,
> Their Heads and Lives, Types of his Chivalry:
>
> . . .
>
> Or shall I tell of his adventures since,
> Done in *Virginia*, that large Continence:
> How that he subdu'd Kings unto his yoke,
> And made those Heathen flie, as wind doth smoke;
> And made their Land, being of so large a Station,
> A habitation for our Christian Nation:
>
> . . .

Smith would have liked that. He would also have been grateful that his friends placed after the poem the simple identification that the yeoman's son had used on the title-page of his own major works. It described the man as he wanted posterity to remember him: "Captaine *John Smith*, sometime Governour of *Virginia*, and Admirall of *New England*."

Some of the controversy that swirled around John Smith during his lifetime continues to the present. Because he was outspoken and aggressive, he made enemies; because he wrote with candor, his writings have enraged some readers while enthralling others. Critics of John Smith contend that he often invented episodes to glorify himself; they warn the reader to view Smith the historian skeptically. His harshest critics go further: Smith, they insist, made only minimal contributions to English colonization and may, in the long run, have done it appreciable harm by providing disruptive and incompetent leadership in Virginia, and by condemning too openly the inadequacies of the London Company when it needed constructive support.

Most of Smith's contemporaries refrained from attacking him in print, although George Percy, William Strachey, and others wrote versions of early Virginia that differed at several points from his. Within only thirty years of his death, however, Smith received a verbal thrashing in Thomas Fuller's caustic *Worthies of England,* published in 1662. "It soundeth much to the diminution of his deeds that he alone is the herauld to proclaim them," Fuller suggested, and he chose to believe very little of what Smith proclaimed. Yet because Fuller's own credentials left something to be desired (his biographical sketches depended more on rumor than on research), the wound to Smith's reputation healed quickly. By 1685 Smith received high praise in a short biography in Latin by Henry Wharton, a distinguished English cleric and passable scholar. Other, and better, biographies followed. During the eighteenth and early nineteenth centuries the captain became something of a folk hero on both sides of the Atlantic.

A sharp turn in Smith's reputation came amidst the passions of the American Civil War. Henry Adams, the distinguished autobiographer and New England patrician, launched his own career as a historian by attacking the south's favorite founder. Advised by John Gorham Palfrey, filiopietistic historian of New England, that an attack on Smith "would attract as much attention, and probably break as much glass, as any other stone that could be thrown by a beginner," Adams raised new doubts about Smith's veracity and reliability. Other northern historians chimed in. Before long it became *de rigeur* to criticize Smith as inaccurate and excessively vain. In the mid-1960s a leading American historian concluded that "John Smith was a liar, if you will, but a thoroughly cheerful and generally harmless liar." Not surprisingly, the public mind remained skeptical about the captain's exploits in Asia and America. It took, after all, almost an act of faith to believe that one man could have lived so dramatic and implausible a life — "which," as his eulogist admitted, "to the World impossible would seem."

Perhaps the skepticism is healthy. We should not be too ready to accept a man's version of his own deeds, nor to forget that in Smith — as in innumerable other men — there was a touch of the braggart and the bully. At the same time, it is unfair to judge Smith only through the eyes of his enemies or to reject his exploits merely because they stretch our credulity. Smith lived in a heroic age. He had one foot firmly planted in the era of brave men and fair damsels, of chivalry and daring, of individual combat, breathtaking rescues, and gruesome trophies. His other foot rested, gingerly but inevitably, in the new age of business corporations and stockholders meetings, of bureaucracy and central government, of collectivity and anonymity. Smith must be measured in light of his times, no matter how unlike our own.

Modern scholarship has demonstrated beyond reasonable doubt the general validity of Smith's historical and autobiographical writings. Bradford Smith made a major contribution to the reappraisal in 1953 with an admirable biography; it included an appendix on the captain's Hungarian escapades that presented solid grounds for believing his account, none for questioning it. More recently Philip Barbour's exhaustive and convincing analysis of John Smith's career and writings lent further credibility to Smith's own version of his life and times.

Which is not to say that John Smith never stretched a tale or told it with an eye to his own place in history. But so far no one has proven him to be anything but what he claimed — a hard-working, hard-fighting soldier who cared deeply about his nation's expansion into the forests of America and who recorded its progress as faithfully as he could. Perhaps for that reason he became a hero in his adopted country. Perhaps, too, in John Smith young America found a prototype of itself: bold, energetic, and optimistic; at the same time brash, intolerant, overly proud of its achievements, and overly solicitous of approval. Such a symbol fit with ease the boundless land, so laden with riches, and the aggressive settlers who conquered it.

A Note on the Sources

TWO SOURCES OF INFORMATION — one a product of the late nine-teenth century, the other of the mid-twentieth — are indispensable to any study of Captain John Smith and his times. In 1884 Edward Arber edited Smith's *Works, 1608–1631* (Birmingham, Eng.), a compendium of all Smith's writings except *A Sea Grammar*. Arber's collection was reissued in Edinburgh in 1910 with an introduction by A. G. Bradley and retitled *Travels and Works of Captain John Smith*. Though not without flaws, the Bradley-Arber edition is still the basic primary source for its subject. In 1964 Philip L. Barbour of Newtown, Connecticut, published *The Three Worlds of Captain John Smith* (Boston). This detailed narrative of John Smith's career in Asia and Europe as well as in America makes Barbour the unparalleled authority on Smith. It is therefore fortunate that several scholarly institutions are sponsoring a new edition of the captain's writings under Mr. Barbour's skillful editor-ship.

Biographies of Smith have run the gamut from children's books to scholarly tomes; not infrequently they have damned or praised him beyond all recognition. Other than Barbour's, the only modern biography of merit is Bradford Smith, *Captain John Smith* (Phila-delphia, 1953); its appendix by Laura Polanyi Striker launched the rehabilitation of the captain's Hungarian career. Older biographical studies that, despite their age, still offer some insight into Smith's life and times are: A. G. Bradley, *Captain John Smith* (London, 1905); E. Keble Chatterton, *Captain John Smith* (New York, 1927); and John Gould Fletcher, *John Smith — Also Pocahontas* (New York, 1928).

Among the primary sources on which my own interpretation rests is Susan Myra Kingsbury, ed., *Records of the Virginia Company of London*, 4 vols. (Washington, D.C., 1906–1935), a treasury of information on the activities of the English and American wings of the Virginia enterprise. Unfortunately, major portions of the company's records have never been found; Miss Kingsbury's compilation includes all that remains of the company's minute books and correspondence. They are quite full for the period from 1619 to 1624, frustratingly sparse for the years 1606 through 1618. Essential supplements to the company records are Philip L. Barbour, ed., *The Jamestown Voyages under the First Charter, 1606–1609*, 2 vols. (Cambridge, England, 1969); Alexander Brown, ed., *Genesis of the United States*, 2 vols. (Boston, 1890; reprinted New York, 1964); Lyon Gardiner Tyler, ed., *Narratives of Early Virginia, 1606–1625* (New York, 1907); and two works by Samuel Purchas: *Purchas his Pilgrimage, Or, Relations of the world* . . . (London, 1613; several subsequent editions), and *Hakluytus posthumus, or Purchas his pilgrimes*, 4 vols. (London, 1625; reissued 1626 with a fifth volume containing *Purchas his Pilgrimage*; 1625 edition reprinted Glasgow, 1905–1907 in 20 vols.). There are many comments on the Virginia venture in Norman Egbert McClure, ed., *The Letters of John Chamberlain*, 2 vols. (Philadelphia, 1939).

Among the most useful and reliable secondary works on early Virginia are Richard L. Morton, *Colonial Virginia, I: The Tidewater Period, 1607–1710* (Chapel Hill, N.C., 1960); three works by Philip A. Bruce, *Institutional History of Virginia in the Seventeenth Century*, 2 vols. (New York, 1910), *Economic History of Virginia in the Seventeenth Century*, 2 vols. (New York, 1895), and *Social Life of Virginia in the Seventeenth Century* (New York, 1907); and two works by Alexander Brown, *English Politics in Early Virginia* (New York, 1901; reprinted New York, 1968), and *The First Republic in America* (Boston, 1898); and Wesley Frank Craven, *The Southern Colonies in the Seventeenth Century* (Baton Rouge, La., 1949).

Useful guides to additional materials are E. G. Swem, John M. Jennings, and James A. Servies, eds., *A Selected Bibliography of Virginia, 1607–1699* (Williamsburg, Va., 1957), which includes both primary and secondary works; and Alden T. Vaughan, ed., *The American Colonies in the Seventeenth Century* (New York, 1971), which lists secondary studies only.

The principal modern sources for understanding the first successful British American colony are listed below, chapter by chapter.

Chapter I: The literature on the age of Elizabeth is vast. Especially
valuable for insights into the mood of the nation, particularly its
growing awareness of the prospects for colonization, are David Beers
Quinn, *Raleigh and the British Empire* (London, 1947), and *England and the Discovery of America, 1481–1620* (New York, 1974);
A. L. Rowse, *The Expansion of Elizabethan England* (New York,
1955), and *The Elizabethans and America* (New York, 1959); D. W.
Waters, *The Art of Navigation in England in Elizabethan and Stuart
Times* (New Haven, Conn., 1958); James A. Williamson, *The Age
of Drake*, 4th ed. (New York, 1960); Louis B. Wright, *Religion and
Empire: The Alliance between Piety and Commerce in English Ex-
pansion, 1588–1625* (Chapel Hill, N.C., 1943); George B. Parks,
Richard Hakluyt and the English Voyages, 2nd ed. (New York,
1961); Theodore K. Rabb, *Enterprise and Empire: Merchant and
Gentry Investment in the Expansion of England, 1575–1630* (Cam-
bridge, Mass., 1967); *The Cambridge History of the British Empire,*
I (Cambridge, England, 1929), chapters 1–6; Samuel Eliot Morison,
The European Discovery of America: The Northern Voyages (New
York, 1971), especially chapters 5–6, and 14–20; S. G. Culliford,
William Strachey, 1572–1621 (Charlottesville, Va., 1965); and
Muriel Rukeyser, *The Traces of Thomas Hariot* (New York, 1970).
Hakluyt's works can be used conveniently in an edition published
in the Everyman's Library series, 8 vols. (London, 1907). The
Roanoke colonies are best described and documented in David Beers
Quinn, ed., *The Roanoke Voyages, 1584–1590*, 2 vols. (London,
1955).

Information on the early life of John Smith comes almost entirely
from his own later recollections, especially in his *True Travels*
(Arber and Bradley, *Travels and Works of Captain John Smith,*
pp. 805–916). The debate on the veracity of Smith's account is discussed in Laura P. Striker and Bradford Smith, "The Rehabilitation
of Captain John Smith," *Journal of Southern History,* XXVIII
(1962), 474–481; and Philip A. Barbour, "Fact and Fiction in
Captain John Smith's *True Travels,*" in Warner G. Rice, ed., *Literature as a Mode of Travel* (New York, 1963).

Chapters II and III: Smith's histories remain the fullest source on
the early years of the Jamestown colony, especially his *True Relation*

(1608) and his *Map of Virginia* (1616), but other important material survives as well. Much of it is collected in Barbour's *The Jamestown Voyages,* and Brown's *Genesis of the United States.* Important too are George Percy, "Observations gathered out of a Discourse . . . ," published in condensed form by Samuel Purchas, *Purchas his Pilgrimes* (1625), IV, 1685–1690, reprinted in Tyler, *Narratives of Early Virginia;* Edward Maria Wingfield, "A Discourse of Virginia," American Antiquarian Society, *Archaeologica Americana* IV (1860), 69–103; and Gabriel Archer [?], "A relayton . . . of the Colony," in ibid., 40–65.

Chapter IV: Most of the materials that pertained to Chapters II and III treat the subsequent few years as well, especially Smith's *Map of Virginia.* Also important are George Percy, "A Trewe Relacyon of the Proceedings and Occurentes of Momente which have happened in Virginia from . . . 1609, until . . . 1612," in *Tyler's Quarterly Historical and Genealogical Magazine,* III (1922), 259–282; and briefer documents reprinted in Brown, *Genesis of the United States;* Barbour, *The Jamestown Voyages;* and Kingsbury, *Records of the Virginia Company.* The charter of 1609 can be consulted most conveniently in Samuel M. Bemiss, ed., *The Three Charters of the Virginia Company of London* (Williamsburg, Va., 1957); first-hand accounts of the wreck of the *Sea Venture* are in Louis B. Wright, ed., *A Voyage to Virginia in 1609: Two Narratives* (Charlottesville, Va., 1964), and R[ichard] Rich, *Newes from Virginia* (London, 1610). Additional information on the colony can be found in *A True Declaration of the estate of the Colonie in Virginia . . .* (London, 1610), reprinted in Peter Force, ed., *Tracts and Other Papers Relating Principally to the Origin, Settlement, and Progress of the Colonies in North America . . .* 4 vols. (Washington, D.C., 1836), III, no. 1. The most thorough description of the starving time is by Percy; additional details can be found in Smith's *Works* and in "A Tragical Relation of the Virginia Assembly, 1624," in Tyler, *Narratives of Early Virginia.*

Secondary accounts that treat this period well are Morton, *Colonial Virginia;* Brown, *The First Republic;* and George F. Willison, *Behold Virginia! The Fifth Crown* (New York, 1951).

Chapters V and VI: In addition to the writings of Smith and Percy, my account of the period from about 1611 through 1617 draws on materials in Brown's *Genesis of the United States*, Robert Johnson's *The New Life of Virginia . . . being the second part of Nova Britannia* (London, 1612; reprinted in Force, *Tracts*, I, no. 7); and especially from Ralph Hamor, *A True Discourse of the Present State of Virginia . . .* (London, 1615; reprinted Richmond, Va., 1957).

The *Lawes Divine, Morall and Martiall* have been published a number of times, most recently as a "Jamestown Document" edited by David H. Flaherty (Charlottesville, Va., 1969). An early analysis of the *Lawes* is Walter F. Prince, "The First Criminal Code of Virginia," American Historical Association, *Annual Report for 1898* (1899), I, 309–363; a more recent and more perceptive interpretation is Darrett B. Rutman, "The Virginia Company and Its Military Regime," in Rutman, ed., *The Old Dominion: Essays for Thomas Perkins Abernathy* (Charlottesville, Va., 1964). Spain's response to the Virginia colony is documented in Barbour, *The Jamestown Voyages;* and more extensively in Irene A. Wright, ed., "Spanish Policy towards Virginia, 1606–1612," *American Historical Review*, XXV (1920), 448–479. John Rolfe's letter to Sir Thomas Dale is in Hamor's *True Discourse* and reprinted in Tyler's *Narratives of Early Virginia*. Rolfe's *True Relation of the State of Virginia . . .* (London, 1617) has been reprinted several times, recently with a biographical introduction by John M. Jennings (New Haven, Conn., 1951).

Insights into Virginia's failures in silk culture and success with tobacco can be found in [John Bonoeil], *Observations To Be Followed, for the Making of fit roomes, to keepe Silke-wormes . . .* (London, 1620) and the same author's *His Majesties Gracious Letter to the Earle of Southampton . . . Also a treatise on the Art of making Silke . . .* (London, 1622); Edward Waterhouse, *A Declaration of the State of the Colony and Affaires in Virginia* (London, 1622); and Samuel Purchas, "Virginia's Verger: Or a Discourse shewing the benefits which may grow to this Kingdome from American English Plantations . . ." in *Purchas his Pilgrimes*, XIX, 218–267. James I's proclamation of 1624 regulating tobacco is in Ebenezer Hazard, ed., *Historical Collections*, 2 vols. (Philadelphia, 1792), 224–230. Helpful secondary accounts include Melvin Herndon, *Tobacco in Colonial Virginia: "The Sovereign Remedy"* (Williamsburg, Va., 1957); Lyman Carrier, *Agriculture in Virginia, 1607–1699* (Williams-

burg, Va., 1957) ; Bruce, *Economic History of Virginia;* and Edmund
S. Morgan, "The First American Boom: Virginia 1618 to 1630,"
William and Mary Quarterly, 3 ser. XXVIII (1971) , 169–198.

Documents relative to the creation and early meetings of the
House of Burgesses are in H. R. McIlwaine, ed., *Journals of the
House of Burgesses of Virginia, 1619–1658/9* (Richmond, Va., 1915)
and in Kingsbury, *Records of the Virginia Company,* III. The
circumstances surrounding the calling of a representative assembly,
and its significance, have been analyzed in W. W. Henry, "The
First Legislative Assembly in America," *Virginia Magazine of History
and Biography,* II (1894) , 55–67; J. A. C. Chandler, *Representation
in Virginia* (Baltimore, 1896) ; Elmer I. Miller, *The Legislature of
the Province of Virginia* (New York, 1907) ; Craven, *Southern
Colonies in the Seventeenth Century;* and most recently in Michael
Kammen, *Deputyes and Libertyes: The Origins of Representative
Government in Colonial America* (New York, 1969) .

Chapter VII: The complicated factional struggles within the
London Company are best approached through Wesley Frank
Craven, *Dissolution of the Virginia Company: the Failure of a
Colonial Experiment* (New York, 1932) , and his more recent pamph-
let, *The Virginia Company of London, 1606–1624* (Williamsburg,
Va., 1957) .

Information on the lotteries is in Brown, *Genesis of the United
States;* Smith's *Works;* Brown's *First Republic; Purchas his Pilgrimes;*
and the *Records of the Virginia Company.* The best secondary treatment is Robert C. Johnson, "The Lotteries of the Virginia Company,
1612–1621," *The Virginia Magazine of History and Biography,*
LXXIV (1966) , 259–292. The changing land policies of the company can be followed in Kingsbury, *Records of the Virginia Company;* and in Bruce, *Economic History of Virginia.*

Scraps of information on attempts to educate and convert the
Indians are in *Purchas his Pilgrimes* and Kingsbury, *Records of the
Virginia Company.* Adequate summaries can be found in Robert
Hunt Land, "Henrico and Its College," *William and Mary Quarterly,*
2 ser. XVIII (1938) , 453–498; and W. Stitt Robinson, "Indian Edu-
cation and Missions in Colonial Virginia," *Journal of Southern
History,* XVIII (1952) , 152–168.

Chapter VIII: The colonization literature of the early seventeenth
century abounds with complaints about the indolent and unruly

settlers. A perceptive modern analysis is Edmund S. Morgan, "The Labor Problem at Jamestown, 1607–18," *American Historical Review*, LXXVI (1971), 595–611. Useful also is Bruce, *Economic History of Virginia*. The importation of brides is discussed in Edward D. Neill, "English Maids for Virginia Planters," *New England Historical and Genealogical Register*, XXX (1876), 410–412, which draws almost exclusively on materials subsequently published in Miss Kingsbury's edition of the London Company's *Records*. Observations on the feasibility of Indian labor can be found in several documents; one of the most explicit statements is in R[obert] G[ray], *A good Speed to Virginia* (London, 1609; reprinted New York, 1937).

Demographic aspects of early Virginia are discussed in Herbert Moller, "Sex Composition and Correlated Culture Patterns of Colonial America," *William and Mary Quarterly*, 3 ser. II (1945), 113–153; and especially in Irene D. W. Hecht, "The Virginia Muster of 1624/5 As a Source for Demographic History," ibid., 3 ser. XXX (1973), 65–92. Important for insights into population growth as well as patterns of land acquisition are Wesley Frank Craven, *White, Red, and Black: The Seventeenth Century Virginian* (Charlottesville, Va., 1971); and Edmund S. Morgan, "Headrights and Head Counts," *Virginia Magazine of History and Biography*, LXXX (1972), 361–371.

Information on the religious and ethnic composition of the colony is scattered through the standard sources. Among the better secondary accounts of the colony's religious growth are Perry Miller, "Religion and Society in the Early Literature of Virginia," in Miller, *Errand into the Wilderness* (Cambridge, Mass., 1956); William H. Seiler, "The Church of England as the Established Church in Seventeenth-Century Virginia," *Journal of Southern History*, XV (1949), 478–508; William Stevens Perry, "The Foundations of Church and State in Virginia," *Historical Magazine of the Protestant Episcopal Church*, XXVI (1957), 34–64; E. Clowes Chorley, "The Planting of the Church in Virginia," *William and Mary Quarterly*, 2 ser. X (1930), 191–213; and the appropriate sections of George MacLaren Brydon, *Virginia's Mother Church* . . . (Richmond, Va., 1947).

Very little of value has been written on Virginia's early social structure, but see Bruce's *Social Life of Virginia*, and Thomas J. Wertenbaker's *Patricians and Plebians in Virginia* (Charlottesville, Va., 1910), *Virginia under the Stuarts, 1607–1688* (Princeton, N.J.,

1914), and *The Planters of Colonial Virginia* (Princeton, N.J., 1922). The literature on the origins and growth of Negro slavery is voluminous and growing. The most important single study is Winthrop D. Jordan, *White Over Black: American Attitudes Toward the Negro, 1550–1812* (Chapel Hill, N.C., 1968). Important also are Oscar and Mary F. Handlin, "Origins of the Southern Labor System," *William and Mary Quarterly*, 3 ser. VII (1950), 199–222; Carl N. Degler, "Slavery and the Genesis of American Race Prejudice," *Comparative Studies in History and Society*, II (1959), 49–66; Thad W. Tate, Jr., *The Negro in Eighteenth Century Williamsburg* (Williamsburg, Va., 1965), chap. I; Paul C. Palmer, "Servant into Slave: The Evolution of the Status of the Negro Laborer in Colonial Virginia," *South Atlantic Quarterly*, LXV (1966), 355–370; Louis Ruchames, "The Sources of Racial Thought in Colonial America," *Journal of Negro History*, LI (1967), 251–272; George M. Frederickson, "Toward a Social Interpretation of the Development of American Racism," in Nathan I. Huggins, et al., eds., *Key Issues in the Afro-American Experience*, I (New York, 1971), 240–254; Craven, *White, Red, and Black;* Edmund S. Morgan, "Slavery and Freedom: The American Paradox," *Journal of American History*, LIX (1972), 5–29; Alden T. Vaughan, "Blacks in Virginia: A Note on the First Decade," *William and Mary Quarterly*, 3 ser. XXIX (1972), 469–478; and Warren S. Billings, "The Cases of Fernando and Elizabeth Key: A Note on the Status of Blacks in Seventeenth Century Virginia," ibid., 3 ser. XXX (1973), 467–474. The primary sources on early slavery are widely scattered.

On Virginia's place in an emerging American society, there is little agreement among scholars. The following are suggestive: Edward Eggleston, *The Transit of Civilization: From England to America in the Seventeenth Century* (New York, 1900); Bruce, *Social Life of Virginia* and *Institutional History of Virginia;* Sigmund Diamond, "From Organization to Society: Virginia in the Seventeenth Century," *American Journal of Sociology*, LXIII (1958), 457–475; Daniel J. Boorstin, *The Americans: The Colonial Experience* (New York, 1958); and Michael Kammen, *People of Paradox: An Inquiry Concerning the Origins of American Civilization* (New York, 1972).

Chapter IX: There is no definitive study of the Indians of the Chesapeake area. Of some value are Charles C. Willoughby, "The

Virginia Indians in the Seventeenth Century," *American Anthropologist,* new ser. IX (1907), 57–86; Frank G. Speck, "Chapters on the Ethnology of the Powhatan Tribes of Virginia," Heye Foundation, *Indian Notes and Monographs,* I (1919), 223–455; Maurice Mook, "The Anthropological Position of the Indian Tribes of Tidewater Virgina," *William and Mary Quarterly,* 2 ser. XXIII (1943), 27–40; and Ben C. McCary, *Indians in Seventeenth Century Virginia* (Williamsburg, Va., 1957). Much of the information about the Virginia tribes comes from Smith's narratives and map.

Early Indian-white relations are analyzed in Wesley Frank Craven, "Indian Policy in Early Virginia," *William and Mary Quarterly,* 3 ser. I (1944), 65–82; Craven, *White, Red, and Black;* Keith Glenn, "Captain John Smith and the Indians," *Virginia Magazine of History and Biography,* LII (1944), 228–248; also Philip L. Barbour, *Pocahontas and Her World* (Boston, 1970); and Gary B. Nash, "The Image of the Indian in the Southern Colonial Mind," *William and Mary Quarterly,* 3 ser. XXIX (1972), 197–230.

The best description of the massacre and its aftermath is in Waterhouse, *A Declaration of the State of the Colony,* but there is extensive additional material in Kingsbury, *Records of the Virginia Company;* Smith's *Works;* and *Purchas his Pilgrimes.* A good modern account can be found in Richard Beale Davis, *George Sandys, Poet-Adventurer* (London, 1955). Evidence of English attitudes toward the Indians prior to the massacre is dispersed through the sermons, pamphlets, and other tracts written on both sides of the Atlantic between 1607 and 1622. Especially revealing are the writings of Robert Johnson, Robert Gray, Patrick Copland, and John Smith.

The collapse of the Virginia Company is thoroughly described and analyzed in Craven, *Dissolution of the Virginia Company;* most of the sources are in Kingsbury, *Records of the Virginia Company.*

Chapter X: What little is known about John Smith's later years comes almost exclusively from his own writings, especially his *True Travels,* supplemented at times by *Purchas his Pilgrimes.* My assessment of Smith as a historian and propagandist relies in part on a reading of his works, in part on the assessments of modern scholars — with whom on the whole I agree but occasionally do not — as presented principally in Barbour's *Three Worlds* of *Captain John Smith,* Bradford Smith's *Captain John Smith,* and Everett Emerson's

Captain John Smith (New York, 1971). I have expressed elsewhere (Alden T. Vaughan and George Athan Billias, eds. *Perspectives on Early American History* [New York, 1973]) my judgments as to Smith's contributions to the evolution of Virginia's historical literature. Here I have tried to fit his writings into the wider canvas of English colonization efforts. As stated earlier in this bibliographical note, the Arber and Bradley edition of Smith's *Works* includes everything the Captain wrote except *A Sea Grammar*. For that volume I have used the informative edition of Kermit Goell (London, 1970), supplemented by Philip L. Barbour, "Captain John Smith's Sea Grammar and Its Debt to Sir Henry Mainwaring's 'Seaman's Dictionary,' " *Mariner's Mirror,* LVIII (1972), 93–101.

Laura Polanyi Striker has translated and edited Henry Wharton's *The Life of John Smith, English Soldier* (Chapel Hill, N.C., 1957). Henry Adams' aspersions appeared in *North American Review,* CIV (1867) and are reprinted in his *Historical Essays* (New York, 1891). Convenient anthologies of Smith's writings are John Lankford, ed., *Captain John Smith's America* (New York, 1967); and David Freeman Hawke, ed., *Captain John Smith's History of Virginia* (Indianapolis, Ind., 1970).

Index

John Smith is abbreviated JS.

Illustration Credits